—THE—
STAN DEFREITAS
GARDEN ANSWER BOOK

Stan DeFreitas

TAYLOR PUBLISHING COMPANY · DALLAS, TEXAS

Published by Taylor Publishing Company
1550 West Mockingbird Lane
Dallas, Texas 75235
www.taylorpub.com

Book design by Mark McGarry
Set in Meridien

Library of Congress Cataloging-in-Publication Data
DeFreitas, Stan.
    The Stan DeFreitas garden answer book / written by Stan DeFreitas.
        p.   cm.
    Includes index.
    ISBN 0–87833–984–1
    1. Gardening—Florida—Miscellanea. I. Title.
SB453.2.F6D47   1998
635'.09759—dc21   98–9964
                                                               CIP

Printed in the United States of America
10 9 8 7 6 5 4 3 2 1

To Peggi and James,
and to all of my loyal television viewers, radio listeners,
and book readers, for their love and support
in all my life's endeavors.

CONTENTS

ACKNOWLEDGMENTS

The author wishes to thank the many fine people responsible for their efforts in reviewing many drafts, adding ideas, and helping to shape my thoughts into a book. Thanks to my wife, Peggi, Karen Hehr, and Allison Walters for putting my ideas to paper and disks. Also, thanks go to the reviewers, Opal Schallmo, urban horticulturist, Pinellas County Extension Service; John Cullen, certified arborist; Jon Wilbur, tree specialist and certified arborist; Mary Coleman, annuals specialist; and Bob Keelor and Chelsie Vandaveer, coordinators, USF Botanical Gardens. Extra special thanks goes to Macy Jaggers, for her quick and diligent efforts to make this book a reality.

INTRODUCTION

Most of my life has been dedicated to helping people excel in gardening. Even as a young boy, my love for plants and living things was obvious to those around me. As I was growing up, I was constantly drawn to people who grew plants or were prolific garden growers. The help they gave me has led me to help others the same way.

Through my years as a county urban horticulturist, I have helped thousands of people with their lawn and garden problems. This assistance has included everything from giving advice about pest problems to sharing information about plant types to helping people improve their growing conditions. Over the past two decades, I have been asked almost every kind of plant-related question.

In this book, I have compiled the most commonly asked questions so that Florida gardeners will have an easy-to-use source to turn to for their plant problems. This book is for all you fellow Floridians who are furthering your quests to become better gardeners.

1

SAND AND SOILS

When Northerners think of soil, they picture dark earth rich in organic matter. But they haven't been to Florida. Here we can't get by without frequent watering and fertilizing, especially when growing flowers and vegetables. Although there are some natives that will perform adequately in our Florida sand without the addition of organic material, the choices that do well are few and far between.

Florida soil varies from clay in the north to sand in Central Florida to a muck-type soil in the south. All, however, tend to be low in essential elements such as nitrogen, manganese, phosphorus, potassium, iron, zinc, and magnesium. It is important to supplement your soil with these elements if you want anything to grow well. It's also a good idea to learn the pH balance of your soil because this influences plant growth by affecting soil bacteria, nutrient leaching, toxic elements, nutrient availability, and soil structure. Your local county extension service can test a soil sample for you and let you know its pH level.

There is as little as 1 percent organic matter in our soil. This fact alone makes it clear that adding organic matter is a must for good growth, whether you are preparing a flower bed or a vegetable garden. So in addition to fertilizing and checking your soil's pH, you also need to supplement with cow manure, peat moss, compost, or other organic material. Preparing your Florida soil for successful plant growth does take work, but the rewards are well worth the effort.

Q I cannot get used to the soil in Florida. Can you help me to be better prepared for growing healthy plants?

A We do use the term *soil* loosely here. The actual term used should be *sandy soil*. Most plants will grow, yes, even in sand. You will need to increase the organic matter in this sandy soil. It has only about 1 percent organic matter, making air and water retention highly limited. Ideal soil contains about 25 percent organic matter, so save those grass clippings and leaves. You can also add Florida, Michigan, or Canadian peat moss. Till this into the soil at a depth of six inches. Remember that in just one year, the Florida sun and our heavy rains will break this organic matter down. So keep adding more.

Q My neighbor insists that the soil is too alkaline. What does this mean and how should I correct this?

A A soil's pH helps you determine how to enrich your landscape base for maximum plant growth. The pH scale goes from 0 (the most acidic) to 14 (the most alkaline). The number 7 on the pH scale is neutral. There are pH meters available for purchase at most garden-nursery stores. Many plants prefer a certain pH. The pH of the soil can also be adjusted; add sulfur to lower the acidity and add dolomite to make the soil more alkaline. (Seven to ten pounds of

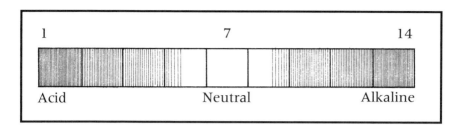

| 1 | 7 | 14 |
| Acid | Neutral | Alkaline |

sulfur per 1000 square feet will lower the pH one unit.) For example, most nurserymen know that plants such as azaleas (*Rhododendron* spp.), camellias, gardenias, and ixoras prefer an acidic soil. Therefore, the pH of 5 to 6 on the scale would be perfect.

 I have beach soil. Should I dig it out and bring in new dirt?

 Adapting and overcoming your soil may be your best choice. For lawn grass, choose a variety that can handle the pH and salt of the beach conditions, such as St. Augustine (*Stenotophrum secundatum*) or Bermuda (*Cynodon Dactylon*). Many palms, such as coconut (*Cocos nucifera*), Chinese fan (*Livistona chinensis*), and Washington (*Washingtonia* spp.), and shrubs, such as oleanders (*Nerium* spp.), beach daisies (*Chrysanthemum* spp.), wedelias, sea oats (*Uniola paniculata*), and sea grapes (*Coccoloba uvifera*), are all good choices. Potting soil mix can be bought for planter boxes or flower beds.

 Should I improve the soil a great deal around my new trees?

 I am a big fan of improving the soil. All flowering beds, vegetable gardens, and small shrubs should have soil amendments added to improve soil conditions. However, larger shrubs and trees need little soil improvements. Many landscapers will save part of the soil from the original planting site of the tree or shrub to be added into the new planting site.

Q In Tallahassee, I am adjusting to a clay soil. What do I use to lighten the clay for planting?

A I practice organic gardening and like many of the ideas used for amending the soil organically. Any yard refuse may be used, such as grass clippings and leaves. Always add organic matter back into the soil, especially if you're trying to lighten it.

Q Each winter, I burn ten to twenty fires in my fireplace. Can I use the wood ash around my plants to help with growth?

A Being a person who enjoys a good fire each winter, I have used the wood ash around my plants for about fifteen years. Wood ash has a good percentage of potash, which is the third element in a fertilizer. This is sprinkled around the base of fruit trees as well as other trees and shrubs. Rake or till it into the ground in the flowering beds or vegetable gardens.

Q I have been reading how beneficial mulch can be for plants. How important is mulching?

A Mulching is a must in the Florida garden, at least most of the time. Any type of mulch material, such as cypress chips, nuggets, pine bark, straw, pine needles, or other recycled organic material, can be used. Many cities provide mulch to the public for free. Contact your local county extension service for details. Mulch helps moderate temperatures, reduces run-off from rain, and has a certain amount of food value that is released into the soil as it breaks down.

Q I have a couple of low spots in my shrub beds and around my elm trees. Can I fill these in to make a smoother, more level ground?

A Changing the grade or level slightly around your shrubs normally will not cause significant problems. Major grade or level change will be detrimental to most shrubs and trees. Most trees' roots will grow in the top twelve to eighteen inches of soil, so oxygen deficiency can occur if too much soil is added around

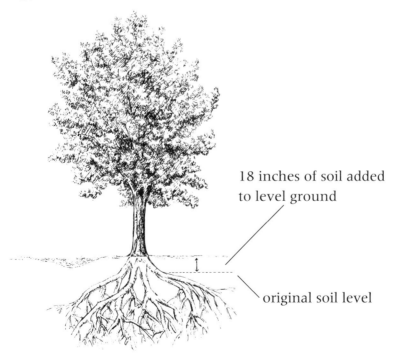

18 inches of soil added to level ground

original soil level

trees. As a certified arborist knows, you must determine the best way to lessen the problems of grade changing. Sometimes local government demands that you change the grade of your property, if this should occur, make sure that you cover no more than 25 percent of the shrub's or tree's root system.

Q My lawn technician told me that my yard should be sanded. What exactly does this mean?

A The old-fashioned idea of sanding the lawn is a practice that has been passed over by most turf growers outside of golf course greens. In this procedure, sand is brought in and spread throughout the lawn area. Although small amounts are acceptable in low areas, large, continued applications of sand will build the turf too high. This will eventually cause problems in thatch build-up, increase the chance of hidden insects and fungus diseases, and will create a problem with mowing.

Q How often should I have my soil tested for pH? Also, how deep should the sample be, and how many samples should I obtain?

A Testing can be done once each season in the vegetable garden as well as in the flowering beds. Most local county extension services offer a pH test for a small fee. I recommend placing your sample in the plastic bag from your local newspaper, then labeling the bag with the areas from which you obtained the sample. For example, you might label it "front lawn (name of grass, if known)," "rose bed," or "vegetable garden." Make sure your sample is from two to six inches in depth. Only one sample per area is needed.

Q Often I hear lectures from horticulturist talking about the fertility of the soil. How important is the fertility of the soil?

A The fertility of the soil is a composite of sixteen essential elements. A lack of any of these elements can inhibit plant growth. In general, most fertilizers will contain macro elements, which are NPK (nitrogen, phosphorus, and potash). They are always measured and recorded in this order, such as a 6-6-6 or 10-12-10. Calcium, sulfur, and magnesium also help make up the macro group. The other elements are considered micro, or trace, elements. These consist of iron, copper, boron, molybdenum, zinc, chlorine, manganese, hydrogen, oxygen, and carbon. All of these elements are interrelated and very important to the soil's fertility.

2

TREES

Almost everyone has some type of attachment to trees. You may remember the tree in your grandmother's backyard that you climbed as a child, or you may have a special tree that you planted at your first new house. Trees play an important role in the feel of your home. And they also have practical advantages, such as cooling your home and lowering your electric bill. The practice of clearing all old vegetation, including trees, off a new homesite is a thing of the past. Today, many people will even pay the extra cost to preserve an old tree on their homesite, and this is a wise investment.

Trees are the slowest growing element in the landscape, but they are also one of the most expensive. Of course, the price depends on the size of the tree you choose. Many people like to purchase a small tree and watch it grow. Others want to see a more immediate effect in their landscape, so they choose a much larger tree. When selecting a tree, keep in mind that you get what you pay for. Cheaper trees are often weak wooded and break down in the first hurricane season. The value of a tree pays off over the years, not just in stately beauty but also in the increased value of your property. As a small tree grows and matures, it can literally become worth hundreds or even thousands of dollars. Wouldn't it be nice if all our investments appreciated at this rate?

Selecting the right tree is of the utmost importance. You will need to find out if the tree you are interested in will fit in with the existing trees in your landscape. Some trees will grow to be large, others very large. Some trees are short-lived, and some are easily damaged in wind storms. These are just a few of the factors you will need to consider when selecting the right tree for your landscape needs. For example, if you want a tree for a certain corner of your backyard, it is important that you find out its ultimate height and width as well as its growing habits. If you don't know how big your tree will become, it may end up taking up more of your neighbor's yard than your own.

Choosing a tree is an important decision that should not be taken lightly. You will be putting quite a bit of money into the tree you select, so be sure you know everything about it. This way you will end up with a good investment that brings years of happiness and beauty to your home.

Q How do I decide how large a tree I should buy?

 A The size of tree you choose will greatly depend on your budget and your landscape needs. If everything in your landscape is small, you might want to select a small tree that will blend in well. However, when starting a new landscape, the trees normally go in first. In this case, many people will put a few dollars more into a good size tree in order to get a more immediate effect in the landscape. Remember, trees are slow growers. If you're buying a young tree, it should be at least one to six inches in trunk diameter. This is measured at standard breast height, usually about four-and-a-half feet from the ground.

Q I used to buy trees for my home sites from field-grown nurseries, but I was recently told these are a thing of the past. Is this true?

A Yes, growing trends have changed. Field-grown nurseries are few and far between today. Most people buy container-grown trees. This makes transporting, transplanting, and the tree's adaptation to growth much easier. If you still buy field-grown trees, get the nurseryman to install it for you; this will minimize the risks during transplanting.

Q Should I put lawn fertilizer in the hole where I will plant my new tree?

A This is not a good idea. You should opt for a mild fertilizer such as milorganite or a time-released, slow-acting fertilizer such as Osmacote. Often a root hormone or stimulator mixed in with a good water-soluble plant food is used. New roots are sensitive, and a lawn fertilizer, which is high in nitrogen, can burn them. Moderation is the key in this situation.

Q Should I plant my new tree at the same depth as the container it came in?

A Definitely. Planting a tree too deeply, or too shallow will cause problems that could eventually lead to the tree's demise.

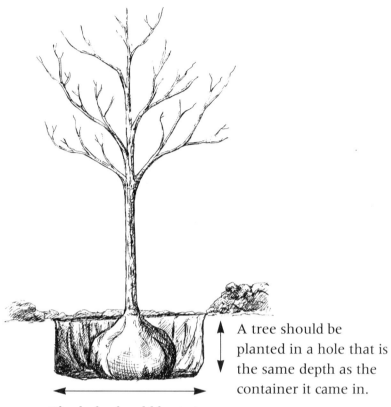

A tree should be planted in a hole that is the same depth as the container it came in.

The hole should be twice as wide as it is deep.

Q How do I know I am buying a good tree at a nursery?

A Most nurserymen try to sell good quality trees. Some things to look for are good color in the leaf, as straight a trunk as possible, and a good healthy root system.

Q My landscape designer seems to have put quite a few trees into his landscape plan. Is it appropriate for me to discuss this with him.

A Of course, you should feel free to consult with the designer you have hired. Most designers like to have a nice, full-looking landscape plan, which is probably why you are seeing so many trees in your landscaper's design. If you can afford this in your budget, you will appreciate having more trees in your landscape in the long run.

Q I was looking at a tree recently that appears to have gone totally dormant during the December-January period. How do I know if there is still life in it?

A Take your thumb nail and scratch the bark. You are looking for life in the cambium layer just underneath the outer bark. This layer should be green and moist

Q Is it safe to transport a tree in the trunk of my car?

A Small trees and plants can be placed in the trunks of cars to save a little money on the nursery's delivery fee. But for a larger plant or tree, it would be worth the extra transporting fee to get your plant or tree home safe and sound. When trees are cramped into trunks, they often experience wind burn and broken branches.

Q I bought a small tree and tried to pick it up by its trunk. When I did this, I pulled the trunk apart from its root system. How should I have picked it up?

A We have all been, at one time or another, guilty of this maneuver. It is best to carry trees by their root ball when moving them around.

Q How quickly should I start watering my newly planted tree?

A As you are planting, have a water hose nearby to spritz the foliage even before removing the tree from the container, especially if it suffered any wind burn during transporting. Immediately after enriching the planting hole with peat moss and refilling it with soil, water the tree deeply.

Q How wide should I dig the hole when planting a new tree?

A Dig the hole twice as wide as you do deep, and be sure to add soil amendments such as peat and other organic matter, making a homogenized mix of the existing soil.

Q We have an old Brazilian pepper tree that we would like to replace with a quality tree, such as an oak. How should we go about this?

A Brazilian pepper trees (*Schinus terebinthifolius*) are quite difficult to get rid of. I recommend cutting the pepper tree down by drilling holes and using a material such as Tordon on the trunk of the tree. You might want to hire a professional pest control operator or certified arborist to help you with this operation. Get rid of the pepper tree before you plant the oak. This way there will not be competition for growth. Also, do not plant you new tree in the same spot as the tree you got rid of. Use a stump grinder to remove as many of the Brazilian pepper tree's roots as possible.

Q We live in a mobile home park. What do you recommend for our small growing situation?

 A There are several trees you can consider: viburnum, holly tree (*Ilex* spp.), dwarf elm (*Ulmus pumila*), redbud (*Cercis canadensis*), and dogwood (*Cornus* spp.). Many of these trees stay small, growing only fifteen to twenty feet tall.

Q We would like to grow a tree in a semiwet area. What kind of tree will grow here?

A It really depends on how wet the area is. Normally, you can use a post hole digger to determine how deep you can dig until you hit water. You might also talk with some of your neighbors and find out what areas hold water and what areas dry out quickly. A water oak (*Quercus nigra*) will grow well in a wet areas. If the area is constantly wet, the bald cypress (*Taxodium distichum*) is a good choice. There are other trees, such as the red maple (*Acer rubrum*) and sweetgum (*Liquidambar Styraciflua*), that will take a good amount of water. Young trees with small root systems will have more problems than existing trees.

Q Are there any trees I can plant here in Florida for beautiful, seasonal color change?

 A Florida certainly does not have the brilliant color changes of New England, but you can see some subtle color changes. Some trees to try include the sweetgum (*Liquidambar Styraciflua*); maples (*Acer* spp.); gingko; crape myrtles (*Lagerstroemia indica*); Chinese tallow (*Sapium sebiferum*); and the golden-rain tree (*Koelreuteria* spp.), which has a yellow bloom in the fall, followed by a papery, pink seed capsule.

Q I noticed a tree being cut in half by a wire that was cutting through its trunk. Does this happen often?

A Typically if a tree is being staked with steel wire, the nurseryman will run the wire through a garden hose first. This will keep it from cutting into the bark of the tree. Sadly enough, many landscapers or maintenance workers do not come back to check on the work. Their job was probably just installation and not upkeep. Unfortunately, the trees are the ones that suffer when jobs are not carefully planned out.

Q I would like to raise my own Fraser fir to use as a Christmas tree. Can this be done successfully here?

A It *can* be done, but it is highly unlikely. A good substitute would be the red cedar (*Juniperus virginiana*) or the Leyland cypress (*Cupressus* spp.). These make nice Christmas trees, but they will not quite be the Fraser (*Abies Fraseri*) fir that is grown up North.

Q Should I worry about removing the burlap that the nursery had my tree growing in?

A It is best to gently cut the burlap away from the roots when possible. True burlap will break down, however, and will not pose a serious problem. But beware, there are many hybrid fabrics used today that have burlap mixed with plastic and other materials that will not break down. If you suspect this is the case, then the burlap should definitely be removed.

Q Should we stake trees when planting?

 A It depends on the size of tree you are planting. At one point, I would have recommended that every tree be staked, but in recent years, there has been evidence that not every tree needs staking. If the tree is not being completely blown over by wind, some movement and interplay with the wind is beneficial to the tree. On the other hand, if the tree seems to be weak, if there is more top growth than root system, or if the tree is leaning to one side, staking is a good idea.

Q I recently purchased a small oak tree and transported it in the trunk of my car. The foliage hung out, and although I didn't go over thirty miles per hour, the leaves are turning brown and falling off. What should I do?

A It is normal for this to happen when you transport a dangling tree. Since the leaves are turning brown and falling off the tree, make sure to give your tree a good watering. You should also build a ring around the tree and keep this area moist. More than likely, new leaves will sprout and grow just fine.

Q When the nurseryman planted a small tree in my yard, he built a ring around it. He said that I should keep it there for some time and eventually tear it down. How long should I wait?

A If your nurseryman has offered a guarantee with the planting of this tree, you may want to confer with him also. Normally, after about three to six months the ring or small mound around a new tree can be removed. At this point, you will have established a regular watering cycle, but you should watch the tree's watering needs closely for the first year.

Q How often should trees be fertilized once they are established?

A As a general rule, trees should be fertilized three times a year: February, June, and October. Many people forget about their trees when they are fertilizing the other plants in their landscape. Trees need attention, too. With enough time, effort, and feedings, you can grow exquisitely majestic trees.

Q We are looking at two oak trees. One has one solid, straight-stemmed trunk, and the other has two major trunks coming out at a point about ten feet up into the tree. Which one should we choose?

A I always advise one to choose the tree with the straight, single trunk. When a tree has multiple trunks coming from the main trunk, there is an increased chance of insect and fungus problems.

Q How good are the spikes I've seen at my local nursery for fertilizing trees?

A The fertilizer spikes are better than not fertilizing the trees at all. They make fertilizing easy and have a good reputation for feeding successfully. Make sure that you do not put the spikes up against the trunk of the tree, and do not go more than eight inches deep because most of the feeder roots will be in that vicinity.

Q We are going to cut a branch off of one of our trees, and this will leave about a four-inch stub. Is this the time to use pruning paint?

A At one time, nurserymen used pruning paint in most instances. Although we do not use it today as much as we once did, it does still have some useful applications. Bad cuts should always be doctored with pruning paint. But, more important, be sure to make a nice clean cut, leaving a shoulder on the wound. This is much more important to the tree's health than applying pruning paint.

Q I recently read an ad for a tree that is supposedly so fast growing that I could get my hammock ready for hanging. What do you know about this?

A You know how the saying goes: If it sounds too good to be true, it probably is. There are trees that grow very quickly, but these are generally weak-wooded. Not only will they not fair well in hurricane season, but they are also not the ideal trees for hammocks.

Q We had a tree hit by lightening. How do we know if the tree will live or even if it is worth saving?

A You might want to hire a certified arborist to come out and look at the tree. He will determine if the tree will live. The tree's chances really depend on whether the tree took a direct hit or just a partial blow. Also, he will determine the value of your tree with a system used by certified arborists. The tree is usually measured at standard breast height (four-and-one-half feet from the ground) and given a replacement value on an inch-per-inch basis.

Q We have a large stump in our yard, and we would like to plant some other plants there but are not sure whether we should try to cover it up or remove it completely. What do you suggest?

A It's best to get a certified arborist to grind the stump down for you. It will take years for the stump to disintegrate on its own. You can try to get rid of it yourself using a product that is poured into holes that you drill in the stump and then ignited. (In some areas, though, burning is not allowed.) Although this do-it-yourself method is an option, the homeowner is frequently unhappy with the results.

Q We have mistletoe growing in our large water oak tree. Is this something to worry about?

A Mistletoe (*Phoradendron* spp.) makes a great conversation piece and is good for kissing under during the Christmas season, but it is a true parasite. The only good control is to have it physically removed, perhaps even cutting out the branches that it has attached itself to.

Q We have a large tree that is draped over much of our house. How worried should we be with the impending hurricane season?

A It might be wise to enlist the services of a certified arborist. Have her check the tree for branches that need to be removed. Trimming some of these heavy branches up and away from the house might be all the protection you will need. A certified arborist is licensed and insured in case problems occur during removal.

Q We have a cavity in the side of our large, stately oak tree. Should we fill it in with mortar or concrete?

Mistletoe growing on a tree.

A Probably not. It is better to clean out these cavities, removing any insects or diseases. Spraying with an insecticide or fungicide is a good preventative measure. Mortar and concrete fillings sometimes impede the tree's own healing process. Also, it can be difficult to know the extent of the diseased part of the tree when these materials are in place. Again, a certified arborist will be able to help you chart a course of action to take for your tree's ultimate health.

Q We have a multitrunked tree that we were told to cable to hold it together. Is this a good idea?

A Cabling is somewhat like surgery—it should be the last line of defense. It should be done by a certified arborist, and the arborist will only decide to employ this method of preservation if it is absolutely necessary for the tree's health. Cabling, like surgery, is expensive and not always necessary.

Q We have a large live oak that has a root growing up near the driveway and appears to be causing a bulge in the sidewalk. What should we do?

A Roots of strong-growing trees can be tremendously powerful. The good news is that these can be safely removed. Doing this on a regular basis (every few years) will prevent recurrences.

Q We planted a Benjamin tree between our house and sidewalk, giving us about three feet in between both. Is this far enough to avoid problems?

A No. As a matter of fact, you will have quite a serious problem someday. Benjamin trees (*Ficus benjamina*) normally grow fifty feet high, and they will spread readily throughout your neighborhood. Although in much of North and Central Florida they will get injured growing outdoors, which will keep them somewhat smaller than they would be if grown in South Florida, you should keep your ficus in a container. This will eliminate any concern about house foundations or damaged sidewalks and driveways.

Q When should I transplant trees in my own yard?

A The best time to do this is during the dormant season, which normally begins at the end of December and continues through early February in Florida.

How often should we water our newly planted tree?

 It is vital to water your new tree every day for the first two weeks to help it adapt to its new location. If you plant it during the hot summer, water it twice a day on those days it does not rain. After the first two weeks have past, continue to water the tree a couple of times a week.

 Is it true that once a tree is established I do not have to feed it anymore?

 No, trees need the sixteen essential elements just like people. If you want to have a healthy, happy tree, feed it on a regular basis. When trees have to survive on what is in the soil, they don't have much chance for proper growth. It may be able to get by on little or no nutrition, but it will pick up insects and disease more readily. Because a tree is one of the biggest investments in the landscape, it makes sense to take care of it properly.

 Is it better to sprinkle a tree on a constant basis or water it deeply a couple of times a week?

 Typically, in Florida we receive about fifty inches of rain a year. If this were spaced out evenly, we would not have to worry about supplementing with extra water. Because this is not the case, you need to water your trees deeply a couple of times a week. This is far better for producing a deeper root system than a constant sprinkling or spritzing program.

Q I've noticed that my neighbor's tree, which is planted in a bed surrounded by shrubs, is growing much better than my tree, which is planted in the middle of my lawn. Why is this?

A Trees tend to grow better when they are planted around other trees and plants. One reason may be that they are benefiting from the attention the other plants are receiving, such as mulching and fertilization.

Q My red maple seems to be having some kind of problem on its twigs. What could this be?

A The red maple (*Acer rubrum*) is prone to attacks by borers to its trunk and, more importantly to you, to the tips of its branches. These are called tip borers, and they can be removed by spraying with Lindane. This can be applied by a certified pest control operator.

Q What is the beautiful tree that has orchidlike blossoms?

A The tree you are describing is the orchid tree (*Bauhinia* spp.). These are small trees, reaching heights of only twenty-five to thirty feet with a spread of fifteen to twenty feet. Orchid trees are not cold hardy and are mostly seen growing in protected areas of Central and South Florida.

Q We have a lovely red maple tree in the front of our property, but there is always some type of sap running from its bark. What causes this?

A Tip borers can be a problem on the tips of red maples (*Acer rubrum*), but even more lethal to these tree are the borers that attack the main trunk. I recommend getting a certified pest control operator, one that specializes in trees, to treat your tree using Lindane in a power sprayer. In addition to the spray application, a certified arborist can inject your tree with a pesticide in capsule form.

Q We have a Brazilian pepper tree. The birds seem to love this tree, although we find it a bit of a nuisance. What do you think of this tree?

A In most cases, I recommend the tree's removal. Besides being a prolific grower that can take over any yard if left unattended, the Brazilian pepper tree (*Schinus terebinthifolius*) has also been reported by some doctors to be the cause of respiratory irritation, headaches, and sneezing. If these factors are not an issue for you, this tree's berries do attract a variety of birds, including redbirds. However, it is illegal to sell or plant Brazilian pepper trees because they are considered exotic invasives.

Q What can you tell me about the bottlebrush?

A As a specimen tree, nothing surpasses the bottlebrush (*Callistemon* spp.) with its vivid red color. It is certainly an excellent choice of a small tree—it grows about fifteen to twenty feet high—to incorporate into the landscape. It is a show stopper with a number of attractive varieties to choose from.

Why isn't the deodar cedar grown more often down here?

 The deodar cedar (*Cedrus Deodara*), which resembles the hemlock (*Tsuga* spp.), does grow well in Florida. It has a lovely pyramidal shape and an attractive blue-green color. The main reason it isn't popular is its slow growth rate. Most nurserymen pass this plant by for faster growing specimens.

 I was told that the redbud is an understory tree. What exactly does this mean?

 An understory tree, such as the redbud (*Cercis canadensis*), grows well underneath a canopy of larger trees. These larger trees are referred to as the overstory. The redbud is one of the smallest understory trees. If your landscape features this forest-type design, the redbud would be a good choice for you.

 We have a Norfolk Island pine that was injured in last year's freeze. How is this possible?

 The Norfolk Island pine (*Araucaria heterophylla*) comes from the tropical Norfolk Islands. Although it looks more like a spruce or hemlock, it is not very cold hardy. In North Florida this tree will get injured every year, which limits its growth to the protected areas of Central and South Florida. If you do live where you can plant this large tree (it reaches heights of sixty feet or more), be sure to allow enough space for it to spread more than twenty feet.

Q Our Norfolk Island pine has some browning on the leaves. What do you think is causing this?

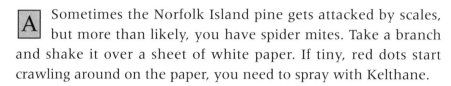 **A** Sometimes the Norfolk Island pine gets attacked by scales, but more than likely, you have spider mites. Take a branch and shake it over a sheet of white paper. If tiny, red dots start crawling around on the paper, you need to spray with Kelthane.

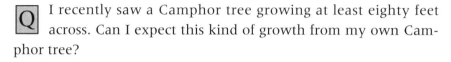 **Q** I recently saw a Camphor tree growing at least eighty feet across. Can I expect this kind of growth from my own Camphor tree?

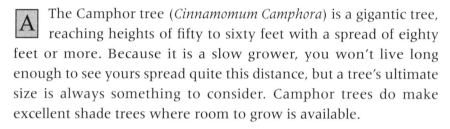 **A** The Camphor tree (*Cinnamomum Camphora*) is a gigantic tree, reaching heights of fifty to sixty feet with a spread of eighty feet or more. Because it is a slow grower, you won't live long enough to see yours spread quite this distance, but a tree's ultimate size is always something to consider. Camphor trees do make excellent shade trees where room to grow is available.

Q How far south can dogwoods be grown?

 A Dogwoods (*Cornus* spp.) grow their best in North and Central Florida. Even in Central Florida, where the dogwood likes a fairly moist soil, it is an understory tree. Dogwoods are ideal specimens, reaching thirty feet high with a twenty-foot spread. They are a delight in the springtime with their showy bracts. The white dogwood can be seen growing further south than the pink variety, which is reserved for North Florida.

Q What type of fertilizer do you recommend for dogwoods?

A An azalea-camellia-type special is the best choice for fertilizing dogwoods. Dogwoods grow best in an enriched, slightly acid soil, and this is an acid-forming fertilizer.

Q My Indian rosewood always seems to be lacking foliage during the cold season. Is this typical for this species?

A The Indian rosewood (*Dalbergia Sissoo*) is considered a semi-evergreen and is a semideciduous tree. This upright tree drops half of its foliage but always seems to have a few leaves hanging on. It can be seen growing in protected areas of Central and South Florida. Although it does get injured in the colder spells of Central Florida, it will normally grow back.

Q On a trip down in the Ft. Lauderdale area, I saw a tree called the silver trumpet. Can I grow this tree in Sarasota?

A The silver trumpet tree (*Tabebuia argentea*) can and does grow well in Sarasota. Just across the Sunshine Skyway from St. Petersburg to the Palmetto area, you can see a wide variety of tropical trees that do not grow well in Pinellas County and farther north. The silver trumpet can be grown further north in a protected site, but they are easily injured by temperatures below 32 degrees Fahrenheit. With its outstanding golden, trumpet-shaped blooms, nothing surpasses this fine tree as a specimen plant.

Q I was told that a royal poinciana once grew in my yard in St. Petersburg, but all I have to show for it is a stump. What happened to it?

A The royal poinciana (*Delonix regia*) is a beautiful tree that can be seen growing mostly in Central and South Florida. There are areas of Central Florida where they get injured by a hard freeze. Most of these trees that grew in Tampa, St. Petersburg, and across the state on the same cold-hardiness map, have been frozen out over the years by cold snaps that reached into the lower teens, which is just too much for this type of tree.

Q I have seen the Australian pine used as hedge material in South Florida. Why isn't it used in other parts of the state?

A The Australian pine (*Araucaria heterophylla*) is native, of course, to Australia. It may look like a cold-hardy variety, but alas, it is not. It was grown farther north at one time, but the hard freezes of 1962, and then again in the '70s and '90s, have limited its growth to a more southern region. As an upright, narrow tree with drooping branches, the Australian pine makes a great wind breaker and street tree.

Q I have heard that the Laurel oak is faster growing than some of the other oaks. Is this true?

A The Laurel oak (*Quercus laurifolia*) is one of the fastest growing oaks. Sometimes described as partly evergreen, it is a much taller than it is wide, reaching a height of sixty feet or more. The Laurel oak is a great choice when you want a fast grower for shade.

Q Our Laurel oak has a pile of sawdust at its base. What makes this mess?

A Oaks in general are tough, but Laurel oaks are more easily damaged by insects than others. The problem you have is borers. Have a certified pest control operator spray with Lindane to get them under control. When a borer problem is caught early and with fertilization, the tree has a good chance for survival.

Q I dearly love the Italian cypress, but it does not seem to be widely grown in Florida. Why is this?

A The Italian cypress (*Cupressus sempervirens*) is typically used as an accent plant—against tall buildings or to frame a large garden, for example. Because there are not many large, formal gardens in Florida, you don't see it growing as much here as in Europe. Growing fifty to eighty feet tall, the Italian cypress does not make a good candidate to be placed up against a one-story Florida home.

Q We saw a fifty-foot tree with pale blue to purple, trumpet-shaped flowers. What is this?

A You are describing the jacaranda tree. These trees are show stoppers when in bloom during May and June. The pale blue to purplish flower, depending upon how long the flowers have been on the tree, literally light the sky with color. This deciduous tree gets injured in North Florida. Also, it is not salt tolerant, so it should be planted inland away from any salt spray.

Q I would like to grow an oak in a slightly moist soil. Which oak can tolerate this?

A The water oak (*Quercus nigra*) grows well in dry soil and fairly moist soils as well. It can reach a height of eighty feet with a spread of about forty feet so allow ample room to grow.

Q Our water oak is on the decline, and I noticed half of a mushroom growing out of the base of its trunk. What does this indicate?

A Your oak has mushroom root rot evidenced by the fruiting body in its final stages. There is not much you can do to control this once the mushroom has appeared. Be prepared to replace this tree.

Q I have heard that the live oak is the best oak to grow in Florida. Is this true?

A Of course the term best is always a matter of opinion, although I do tend to agree. Not only does the live oak (*Quercus virginiana*) reach heights between sixty and one hundred feet, but it will also have a spread of about the same. Because of this growth habit, it makes an outstanding shade tree. It is also slower growing, which means the wood is harder and more resistant to borers and other problems.

Q Will the golden-rain tree grow in North Florida?

A Many flowering trees do not grow well in North Florida, but the golden-rain tree (*Koelreuteria formosana*) is an exception.

It does have beautiful golden blooms, and some people will call it the pink flowering tree because of its pink, papery seed capsules.

Q I'd like to plant a tree that is slightly bigger than a maple but has a beautiful pattern similar to a maple's on its leaves. What tree would you suggest?

A Try the sweetgum (*Liquidambar Styraciflua*) tree, which can be grown in North, Central, and South Florida. The sweetgum gives us one of the best leaf color changes in the fall, much better than the maples in Florida. In fact, when people see them in color change, they often mistake them for maples. Because it is a second cousin of the maple tree, the leaves look quite similar. The only difference is that they are a little larger and have five lobes.

Q My neighbor planted a sweetgum, and the seed pods, which are round, spiny balls, are difficult to walk on. Do all sweetgums have these?

The spiny seed pod of the sweet gum.

Unfortunately, yes. All of the sweetgums have these spiny seed pods. This is the only drawback to growing this wonderful tree.

Q I thought the Chinaberry tree was popular in Florida, but I rarely see it used these days. Why is this?

A The Chinaberry tree (*Melia Azedarach*) was loved by the early Florida pioneers because it grows quickly, providing fast shade. And it does have beautiful blossoms. However, like many other fast-growing trees, it's weak-wooded and does not fair well in wind storms. Another disadvantage to this tree is the mess it leaves with its little yellow seed pods. Just as air conditioners replaced a good cool breeze, the Chinaberry was replaced by stronger growing trees.

Q Our builder planted some wax myrtles for us a few years ago, but most of them have died. What happened?

A Wax myrtles (*Myrica cerifera*) were overused for many years. It is a native tree that was frequently planted in the wrong growing conditions throughout the state. They are not well adapted to constant irrigation and conditions of lawns and gardens.

Q I really like the peltophorum because of its yellow jacaranda look. What can you tell me about it?

A The peltophorum does resembles the jacaranda; so much in fact, that some Floridians call it a jacaranda. Like every tree, it has its pros and cons. First, it is a fast-growing tree, which makes it weak wooded. Also, when their jacaranda-looking blossoms fall off, they cause quite a mess. Reaching heights of fifty or sixty feet, the peltophorum can be too tall for most Florida yards. However, where ample room is available, it does have attractive, delicate foliage.

Q My slash pine is oozing sap from about three feet up its trunk. What does it have?

A Pines are commonly injured by borers and engravers, including beetles. If your problem is in an isolated area, a certified pest control operator can spray with Lindane. But in some situations where an entire block is attacked at once, the only solution is to remove the trees and replace them with a different type of tree.

Q We have a pond, and we would like to plant a tree down into the water. I have seen a graceful tree planted like this in movies. What am I thinking of?

A You are probably talking about the weeping willow (*Salix babylonica*), which is a good tree for wet areas. They are often seen growing in ditch banks. The weeping willow will give you the graceful, flowing branches you desire and make a peaceful setting.

Q I have heard that the Chinese tallow has been restricted from growth in certain communities. Is it really that messy?

A Each community has its own standards. The Chinese tallow (*Sapium sebiferum*) does drop a lot of seeds and spreads easily, often where you don't want it to. But it is also a very attractive tree because when it drops its foliage, the leaves are red, yellow, and wine colored. The Chinese tallow will grow in North, Central, and South Florida.

Q My Jerusalem thorn is not only thorny but also has some scales on some of its stems. What do I use to get rid of these?

A Scales are a problem for many shrubs and trees. Spraying with Cygon or Orthene should help get them under control.

Q How tall will my magnolia tree get?

A The southern magnolia tree (*Magnolia grandiflora*) can be huge, reaching heights of seventy-five to one hundred feet, but its average height is between forty and sixty feet. The beautiful, large (sometimes four to eight inches across) white blossoms and lovely fragrance make this stately tree one of the true aristocrats of the Southern garden.

Q Our magnolia's leaves have brown spots on them. What does it have?

A It has a leaf-spotting fungus, which is not uncommon on the magnolia. Spraying with neutral copper should help. The magnolia is also prone to scales. These can be controlled by spraying with Malathion or Orthene according to label directions.

Q I recently saw a sweet bay tree. What can you tell me about it?

A The sweet bay (*Magnolia virginiana*) grows more upright than some trees, reaching a height of anywhere between fifteen and sixty feet. This tree will grow as tall as it needs to in order to reach the sunlight. It is admired for its beautiful magnolia-type blossoms that are more open than those of the traditional southern magnolia. Although these blossoms are not quite as large, they do have a pleasant fragrance. The sweet bay is often used in avenue plantings and at camp grounds.

3

LAWNS

When choosing a Florida grass, it is best to stick with one of the warm-season grasses: St. Augustine (*Stenotaphrum secundatum*), Bahia (*Paspalum notatum*), Bermuda (*Cynodon Dactylon*), or centipede (*Eremochloa ophiuroides*). The comment "I used to pull that out as crabgrass" is often heard of the St. Augustine varieties popular in Florida. St. Augustine is a runner grass that tolerates the heat and moisture levels in Florida and adjusts well to our soil types. You can start a St. Augustine lawn using plugs, sprigs, or sod. There is no commercial seed for this lawn grass. Although it takes slightly more care than Bahia, and certainly more irrigation, St. Augustine is the grass of choice for most Florida lawns.

Bahia is a great grass for low-water areas. Both the Argentine and Pensacola varieties grow well here, but they do have major problems with the mole cricket. Bahia can be started from either seed or sod, but the more popular method is sod because the seed is difficult to germinate. Germination of seed occurs during warm months and when watered daily. Although it is not the best choice for your lawn, Bahia works well for baseball fields, parks, church grounds, and other areas where an irrigation system is absent.

Bermuda is the grass used on most golf courses. This may sound appealing, but remember, golf courses are fertilized heavily and manicured daily—not really practical for a lawn. There are also weed and nematode problems with Bermuda grass.

Centipede is a dwarf St. Augustine used mostly in Central and North Florida. This grass does not look good in a high pH, or alkaline, soil, which is what you find in South Florida and parts of Central Florida.

For a temporary lawn grass, winter rye (*Secale* spp.) can be used. This is usually seeded in October through November. Rye does die out in May, but it blocks out weeds and, as it dies out, gives food value back to the soil.

Zoysia (*Zoysia Matrella*) is another grass grown in Florida. Under controlled conditions, it makes a good lawn grass. With its fine blade, zoysia resembles Bermuda. Many of our theme parks use zoysia successfully. Of course, theme parks have teams of people who work just in the lawn and plant-care division—this should give you an idea of the amount of attention it demands. Zoysia has its fair share of problems with nematodes. To help keep this problem at bay, most people use a nematicide or use a layer of shell or other sub-based material before planting the zoysia on top. Another disadvantage to zoysia is that it is slow to fill in. All and all, it is a better grass of choice for northern states. Here, zoysia is just too high maintenance for most people.

So, although St. Augustine is not the only choice for the Florida lawn, for most homeowners it is the most practical and the most successful.

 I have noticed my St. Augustine lawn is putting up seed heads. Will these germinate?

A This seed is not considered viable, although under lab conditions a small amount of seed could be germinated. Plugging and sodding are two methods to get a good St. Augustine (*Stenotaphrum secundatum*) lawn.

Q My St. Augustine lawn is thick and squishy to walk on. Someone suggested that I have it verticut. What does this mean?

A Verticutting is done with a special machine called a verticutter. It is similar to a mower, but it has vertical blades spaced about three inches apart. This allows it to cut through the grass runners and slice evenly into the top of the root system, which helps in stimulation and aeration of the grass and soil.

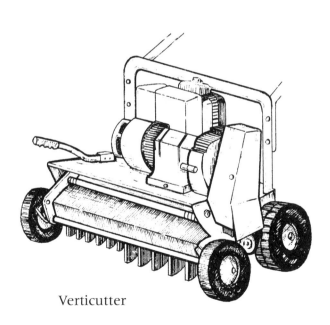

Verticutter

Q Is aeration good for my Bahia lawn?

A Yes. You can use an aerator, power rake, or verticutter. Remember, what you're trying to do is thin and aerate your lawn, not till it like with a rototiller. After thinning, I recommend an application of fertilizer, such as a 16-4-8 analysis, followed by ample watering. This will help produce healthier turf.

Q My lawn is well established. How often do I need to water to get a nice green, healthy looking lawn?

A Although your lawns receive some moisture from rain, condensation, and morning dew, you cannot rely on these methods. Watering once or twice a week with a one-half to one-inch application will develop a stronger and deeper root system. An early morning watering, when the temperature is moderate, will give you the best results.

Q My neighbor said that it was good to spritz a lawn daily. What is your opinion?

A You never want to merely spritz your lawn; instead, you want to water deeply. To determine how much water your lawn is receiving, I recommend using a rain gauge or a moisture meter. Both can be purchased at most garden supply stores.

Q A few of my neighbors have green lawns all winter long. What are they planting in order to have this year-round color display?

A Your neighbors have gotten wise to seeding rye grass (*Lolium* spp.), often sold as winter rye. It is planted in early October in Florida at a rate of five to fifteen pounds per one thousand square feet. Remember, you still have to mow year-round, too.

Q I have spent hours pulling a weed out of my lawn, but unless I constantly keep checking and pulling, it takes over the entire lawn. Can you tell me what it might be and how I can kill it without harming the grass?

A You are undoubtedly talking about southern crab grass (*Digitaria* spp.). In Floratam lawns, I recommend spraying with Asulox, and in Bahia (*Paspalum notatum*) lawns, square off an area and spray with Round-Up. Remember, Round-Up is an equal opportunity killer, so spot treating is recommended.

Q We have a Bahia lawn that the previous owners left overwatered and too high. How high should we cut it and when is the best time to do this?

A Bahia should be cut at a height of two to three inches. Bahia is normally power raked in the spring along with fertilizing.

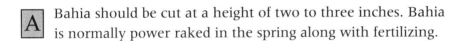

Bahia grass should be cut two to three inches high.

41

Q I was told my lawn has brown patch fungus. What should I do for it?

A Brown patch fungus is an all-too-common problem in Florida lawns. Spraying with Fore or Daconil, using a couple of applications, should help keep the fungus under control. Cutting the lawn too short could be the cause of the problem. Most St. Augustine (*Stenotaphrum secundatum*) varieties should be mowed to about two or three inches in height.

Q Wild Bermuda is taking over our lawn, and we seem powerless to control it. What should we do?

A Wild Bermuda (*Cynodon Dactylon*) is a difficult weed to control. In a Floratam or St. Augustine lawn, good results have been met by using Atrazine. Also, a certified pest control operator can apply a product called Asulox. The combination of these two chemicals seems to take care of wild Bermuda.

Q A creeping beggarweed is growing between two of my oak trees, preventing my St. Augustine from spreading. Do I have to dig it up or should I just throw more sod and hope it is able to overtake it?

A The large creeping beggarweed (*Desmodium tortuosum*), which has a three-leaf clover and a seed part that is quite sticky, is best fought with Atrazine. It may take more than one application to bring the weed under control, but be careful not to overuse weed killer. This can cause even more problems than the weeds. Always read the directions on the label and follow them precisely.

Q I have a running-type weed with sharp, pointy, white roots that is taking over my lawn. What is it and how do I get rid of it?

A You are plagued with the extremely tenacious torpedo grass (*Panicum repens*). I have literally seen this weed grow down underneath a sidewalk and come back up on the other side. I have even seen it grow through large oak roots. Most herbicides will kill this grass back to the joint, or node, but then it will grow again. A number of applications throughout the year will lead to its eventual eradication.

Q We have a very dry area in our lawn. Is there a grass particularly suited for these conditions?

A Most of our southern grasses will take the heat, but dry is a different matter. For this, Bahia (*Paspalum notatum*) is the best choice, both the Argentine and Pensacola varieties. Bermuda is a close second for tolerating dryness. They will go off-color without adequate supplies of water, but they resurrect themselves after the first good rain. It is generally not a good idea to put grass into that type of stress, but if you are unable to keep the area wet enough, Bahia and Bermuda are the best choices.

Q We have some beautiful oak trees, but they make growing grass a problem. Which grass should we plant in their shade?

A It is difficult to grow grass in shady areas because, like all plants, grass develops food in its leaves and this requires sunlight. But sometimes this cannot be avoided, and the best grass for shade is St. Augustine (*Stenotaphrum secundatum*). The best varieties are the Floratine, Seville, or one of the other new varieties

A bed of Boston ferns growing under an oak tree.

that have been adapted to lower light levels. St. Augustine is fairly vigorous and will spread if it gets four to six hours of filtered light during the day. If you have a little more light available and you want the finer look of Bermuda, zoysia (*Zoysia Matrella*) would be the right choice. It will tolerate a lower light than Bermuda but does not quite have the tolerance of the St. Augustine varieties. In areas of extremely dense shade, beds of the Boston fern (*Nephrolepis exaltata* cv. 'Bostoniensis'), creeping fig (*Ficus pumila*), or ivy (*Hedera* spp.) can be used in border-type plantings with lawn grasses farther out from the overhang of the tree.

Q I was visiting a relative who had a Bermuda lawn, but she called it a Tifton lawn. How does Tifton Bermuda differ from regular Bermuda?

A Basically, Bermuda (*Cynodon Dactylon*) is Bermuda. Tifton Bermuda was developed in Tifton, Georgia, through the

USDA program. It is a hybrid Bermuda that is often chosen for its strength and beauty. There are a number of different varieties that have been adapted from this original source. Although the Tifton Bermuda grass provides a somewhat nicer appearance, it will require more maintenance, which means more money.

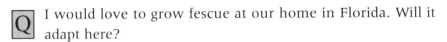 I would love to grow fescue at our home in Florida. Will it adapt here?

In general, cool-season grasses such as fescue and bluegrass (*Poa* spp.) that do well up North do not tolerate the heat and dryness of our summers very well. Maybe someday a fescue (*Festuca* spp.) will be developed for Florida, but for now I recommend sticking with the warm-season grasses such as St. Augustine, Bermuda, Bahia, or Zoysia.

 We are thinking about having a centipede lawn installed at our new home in North Florida. Will it do well here?

You are exactly right. In the panhandle area and much of North Florida, centipede lawn grass (*Eremochloa ophiuroides*) is be a viable lawn choice. Centipede resembles a dwarf St. Augustine in appearance and growth habit. It is a slow grower and tends to yellow out somewhat in higher pH soils, but luckily, in North Florida the soil tends to be more acidic.

We are planning on putting in a new lawn. Is there a recommended month to do this?

Not really. Sodding is done just about year-round. There are some restrictions for seeding certain types of lawns, but sodding and plugging can be done any time. You might want to take advantage of the cool season, when there will be less irrigation requirements. In the middle of summer, new plugs have to be watered twice daily. With this same grass in the fall or winter season, once a day is sufficient to establish new turf.

Q We just put in a new St. Augustine lawn in our backyard. I was told not to mow it right away. Why is this?

A Mowing too soon tends to pick up too much sod, scalping certain pieces. You should find that after a week to ten days, the sod has rooted itself. When the grass has grown to mowing height, by all means mow. As the top of the grass blade is mowed down, it will help to make the sod spread. This is especially true with St. Augustine varieties.

Q We are planning on sodding our new lawn. Is there any fertilizer that we should apply before the sod is put down?

A It is a good idea to use a root-stimulator fertilizer or a non-burning fertilizer such as Milorganite underneath newly planted grass. Milorganite will give some food value without the root burn. You might also want to sprinkle a light application of a quality fertilizer on top once the sod is laid. There are pros and cons to fertilization, but in general, a light application of fertilizer is helpful in establishing lawn grass.

Q My Bahia yellowed somewhat after a recent fertilization. What caused this?

A It is not uncommon for Bahia (*Paspalum notatum*) to experience a false iron deficiency. In other words, when the grass really starts to grow, iron is not assimilated by the Bahia as well as it should be. This problem normally works itself out in about two weeks, and the yellowing disappears.

Q Should I water my lawn in the early morning or the late afternoon?

A Early morning watering is preferred. Morning watering is not lost through the evaporation of the sun as quickly. Watering in the late afternoon requires you to run the water for too long, which increases fungus potential—although usually the fungus will adapt and problems can occur no matter when you water.

Q We would like to put new sprinkler heads up near our home, but we do not want the water near the base or side of the building. Are there special heads for this?

A There are a number of different head patterns available at most nurseries and garden supply stores. Some distribute the water over 360 degrees, while others only cover 180 or even just 90 degrees. An irrigation specialist can help you find the right sprinkler head for your situation.

Q We have an automatic irrigation system, which is nice, but the heads often get clogged. Is there any solution to unclogging the heads?

A Debris from leaves and other substances can clog sprinkler heads. Ideally, you should clean them on a monthly basis. Take them apart, remove the debris, and put them back into the pipe. This is not a difficult task, but many people prefer to have an irrigation specialist come on a regular basis to check the system to make sure it is running properly and "blow" the system out.

Q For years I have used a 6-6-6 fertilizer on my lawn, but I have heard you mention a 16-4-8. What is the difference and which should I use?

A My preference for using a 16-4-8 fertilizer is simply that it will go farther. The number 6-6-6 indicates that it contains six pounds of nitrogen, phosphorus, and potassium each in a one hundred-pound bag. Since most of us buy fertilizer in fifty-pound bags, there is only three pounds of each of these three elements in this bag. That's only nine pounds of fertilizer and forty-one pounds of filler. A more concentrated fertilizer will go farther. You also need to determine what a fertilizer is derived from. Some of the cheaper fertilizers are derived from elements that do not last long in the lawn. Other fertilizers, which may be more expensive, contain true organics with a better blend and size.

Q I try to fertilize my shrubs in spring, summer, and fall. Should I follow this schedule for my lawn?

A It really depends on what type of lawn you have. If you are growing a hybrid Bermuda (*Cynodon Dactylon*), you could be fertilizing six to eight times a year, but if you have a Bahia (*Paspalum notatum*) or St. Augustine (*Stenotaphrum secundatum*), three times a year may be adequate for good growth and color. As you mention, applications in spring (February-March), summer (June-

July) and fall (August-September-October) are the minimum for fertilizer.

Q After fertilizing, a downpour drenched our lawn. Is this fertilizer being washed away?

A Absolutely not. A good shower will help push the fertilizer down into the root zone. In fact, before a heavy rainfall is the perfect time to fertilize. However, because you can't always trust the weather forecast, you should always water your lawn after fertilizing.

Q My husband recently fertilized using an old drop spreader. Afterward, I noticed a lot of lines of light and dark colors. What can we do to prevent this from happening with the next fertilization?

A The drop spreader was a popular tool at one time, but the rotary spreader is quicker and easier—and there is much less chance of getting the zebra effect you witnessed.

Q We bought a number of bags of fertilizer on sale, but after months on the garage floor, they are now hard as a brick. Can these still be used?

A Fertilizer is properly stored up off the concrete floor where it can draw moisture over a long period of time. You might try using a hammer to break it back into small particle sizes. Even if you can't get the fertilizer small enough to fit through a spreader, your shrubs and trees can still take advantage of these chunkier pieces.

Q I have read about a weed-and-feed product. Will this really do the job on my St. Augustine lawn?

A Weed-and-feeds can be helpful, especially on a St. Augustine lawn. The weed-and-feed Atrazine is particularly successful with weed eradication in St. Augustine. Yet the weed-and-feed for Bahia, which contains 2,4-D, has not proven that successful. My preference is to mix a weed killer and spray it according to label directions. The tough weeds—dollar weed (*Crassula argentea*), sedges (*Carex* spp.), and the like—will not respond well to weed-and-feeds.

Q Recently I spoke with someone about my dollar-weed problem, and he said it was due to over watering. Does this sound right?

A Yes. Dollar weed is a water weed. Too much irrigation is definitely a contributing factor. Once it is established, cutting back on the water will not necessarily make the dollar weed disappear. Weed killers will be of some help, but be prepared for this to be a perennial problem in your lawn.

Q I have found that this Florida sand you call soil has a tough time holding fertilizer. What amount do you recommend I use on my Florida lawn?

A This will vary with the type of lawn you have. You are right: Florida sand does not hold nutrients in well. It is difficult to add enough amendments to a lawn to make much difference. Therefore, it is better to fertilize with a reduced amount more frequently than trying to overpower the lawn with a heavy fertilization.

 When I finish mowing, my lawn takes on a ragged, gray, dull look. What's the problem?

 You should check your mower to see how sharp the blade is. For a few dollars, most mowing shops will remove the blade and sharpen it with a special grinder. More lawns are killed from dull blades than from insect problems.

 We tend to mow our St. Augustine lawn every seven days during the growing season. Is this adequate?

 Normally, mowing every seven days is adequate for our southern lawn grasses. In general, the rule is to remove only about one third of the grass blade. In reality, this is difficult because of heavy spurts of growth, rainy days that impede mowing, and a host of other potential delays. During the cooler months, every few weeks to once a month is adequate if you have not overseeded with winter rye.

4

SHRUBS

Shrubs are more than the evergreen plants that you might think of, and they are more than just the plantings we place around the house to frame it. In Florida, we have both evergreen and flowering shrubs. Although many people still plant them in rows in front of the home, shrubs are also used to soften the lines of buildings, and large shrubs can be used to fill in the corner of a building. They are considered foundation plantings but can also be used to color the landscape.

Pay close attention to your climate when selecting shrubs. Whether or not a shrub is cold hardy or tolerates the sun well should be considered before planting. Before purchasing your shrubs, you will also want to consider mixing tropicals and evergreens. This will produce a smoother, more eye-appealing effect. Robert Frost said "Good fences make good neighbors." Mr. Green Thumb says, "Good neighbors plant hedges." They help to define your property and increase your privacy by blocking views and creating more intimate areas.

Q A ligustrum hedge that has been growing around my home for a long time has developed spots on the leaves. What causes this?

A If the spots on your ligustrum hedge are yellow or brown, the likely culprit is fungus. You can determine if this is your problem by using a hand lens and searching for tiny dots, which are the spores of a fungus. If you still cannot distinguish the problem, you can take a small branch sample to your local county extension service office or a good quality nursery. If, however, you did see these small spore dots, you'll want to spray with neutral copper.

Q I want to really prune my shrubs back drastically. Is this a good idea?

A It is normally advisable to cut back shrubs only by about 50 percent or so. Trimming out 20 to 30 percent is the range

Cut your shrubs back 20 to 30 percent.

most recommended. Power trimmers make the job much easier, but it is easy to get a little carried away with power tools. Hand trimming helps avoid stubs and notches, allowing the hedges natural beauty to be showcased. All shrubs should be trimmed on occasion just to prevent them from growing out of bounds.

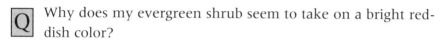 **Q** Why does my evergreen shrub seem to take on a bright reddish color?

A When evergreens turn this color, spider mites are almost always present. Shake a branch onto a sheet of white paper. If you see tiny, reddish-brown dots, you will have to treat with Kelthane or any good miticide. This can also be sprayed on the arborvitae (*Thuja* spp.), Italian cypress (*Cupressus sempervirens*), and other junipers (*Juniperus* spp.).

Q Why do some crape myrtles have only a couple of straight trunks while others have numerous multitrunks?

A By nature, crape myrtles (*Lagerstroemia indica*) tend to be multistemmed shrubs. With a little pruning, they can be formed into small to medium trees. To do this, allow the shrub to grow up to five or six feet, then select the best trunks and remove the extra trunks and side branches. Eventually, you will get the tree-type shrub you desire.

Q Where can I find the jatropha bush?

A The jatropha (*Jatropha integerrima*) bush is a native of Cuba and can be found at specialty nurseries. The jatrophas are not common plants grown in this area. There are about 150 species, the intergerrima being just one of them. Many jatrophas are particularly hardy and strong. They seem to grow well in the lower Central to South Florida areas. The jatrophas should be protected like their second cousin, the poinsettias (*Euphorbia* spp.).

Q We just moved here and have two arborvitaes about five feet tall. They appeared healthy but have recently started dying (browning) out. This die-back starts at the base of the stems and gradually works its way out toward the ends. The needles are dropping and the browning is becoming quite obvious. The arborvitaes are approximately eight years old and looked lovely outside our house. What can I do to make them healthy again?

A This is a fungus problem called juniper blight. You will need to treat it with liquid or neutral copper. It may take a couple of applications seven to ten days apart to get the problem under control. Often the inner portion of the arborvitae will be brown, and this is normal.

Q I have a shrub in my yard that had purple flowers, but it got frozen in the winter. It grew back in the spring, but it has never bloomed again. I am fertilizing, and overall its appearance is healthy. How can I get this plant to bloom again?

A It sounds like you are describing the Princess Flower (*Tibouchina semidecandra*), sometimes called Glorybush. It has beautiful dark-green leaves with three to five main parallel veins reaching up to five inches long. Its gorgeous purple flowers bloom throughout the summer and fall. After a severe freeze (about 30 degrees Fahrenheit), the Princess Flower goes through a period as long as six months to a year without flowering.

Q The leaves on our viburnum hedge have developed brown and white spots. Several bushes have already died. Can you help us?

A Your sweet viburnum (*Viburnum odoratissimum*) has a leaf-spotting fungus. Applying a fungicide such as Dithane M-45 or neutral copper should help. Use three or four applications seven to ten days apart. Also, a good fertilizer applied three times a year should be part of your regime.

Q I thought my azalea leaves were having trouble with mites, so I was using Malathion to help keep them under control. Then a local nursery told me it wasn't a spider mite problem but a lace bug attack. What do I use now?

A The lace bug is normally detected by the use of a magnifying glass. These light-colored, unique-looking insects are so tiny, only 4mm long, that they are difficult to detect. Besides azaleas (*Rhododendron* spp.), they commonly attack verbena (*Lantana* spp.), sycamore, hibiscus, and oaks (*Quercus* spp.). They are best controlled by spraying with Diazinon. It normally takes a couple of applications to bring this problem under control.

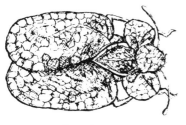

lace bug   spider mite

Q My pittosporum hedge leaves are in various stages of yellowing and dropping off. They also have black spots on the large leaves, although new leaves are green and healthy. What is this and how do I treat it?

A Your pittosporum is suffering from two problems. One is a fungus the other is the Florida wax scale. To control the fungus, use a fungicide such as Daconil. Since the two treatments you need are compatible, you can spray for the wax scale with an insecticide such as Malathion or Diazinon within the same sprayer applicator. It may take seven to ten days to get both of these problems under control.

Q I have a beautiful gardenia bush, full of buds and healthfully green except that some of the leaves are turning yellow and falling off. I used an azalea fertilizer about a month ago. Was this the cause?

A Your gardenia has a deficiency. In April, it is not uncommon to see a few yellow leaves on the gardenia. As it goes into its flowering period, the gardenia will require more water. A couple of waterings per week with a total of about one inch of water should be adequate. Of course, this depends upon the type of soil and how large the bush is. A nutritional spray such as Perk would be helpful. It would also be a good idea to test your soil for acidity. To add more acid use sulphur or a soil acidifier. Your local county extension service can help you with this test.

Q I have five Formosa pine azaleas that were planted seventy-five feet from the sea wall, far enough away to escape any salt spray. They receive about two hours of full sun in the morning, but they still do not look healthy. Any suggestions?

A Seventy-five feet from a sea wall is potentially close enough to get injured by the salt spray. On a windy day, often the salt spray will be picked up and carried some distance. Azaleas (*Rhododendron* spp.) have a very poor salt tolerance and should be planted in an enriched, moist soil. Also, there should be a slight drying between waterings.

Q What is wrong with my gardenia bush? They start to grow nicely but soon begin to look unhealthy.

A Gardenias, like azaleas, prefer an acid soil. When growing in an alkaline pH, sufficient nutrients are often not available. Fertilize with an azalea-camellia special or an acid-forming fertilizer. Keep in mind that it is not uncommon to have a few yellow leaves on the bottom of the plant, especially during the blooming period, and gardenias require quite a bit more water during the blooming season.

Q On the west wall of our home, a podocarpus that receives about a half a day's sun has a black substance on its older leaves. Another podocarpus, about four feet away receives more sun and does not have this appearance. Why is this?

A Planting podocarpus in full sun helps to dry off the morning moisture, thus preventing mildew and other predators of such conditions from attacking. The black sooty mold found on your podocarpus leaves indicates a problem, most likely aphids. They can be combated by spraying with Malathion or Diazinon. It may take a second application in seven to ten days to catch the next generation of aphids.

Q The Men's Garden Club in my area presented me with an unidentifiable plant. The sample of leaves and berries were said to be that of the ant plant. It does have bulbous roots. I am hoping that it is not poisonous because I have small children. How does it propagate?

A The plant commonly known as the ant plant is from the *Rubiaceae* family. A native of Malaysia, it is an epiphytic shrub. The ant plant has green, fleshy leaves with a bulbous base, growing four or five inches across. It has white flowers with red berries when grown under good conditions. The tuberous base is often tunneled out by stinging ants in Malaysia. I would not recommend eating this plant, although it does not seem to be toxic. The ant plant can be started from seed or by division.

Q I have a plant that has grown fourteen feet in the last three weeks. It seems to have come out of nowhere. Should I allow it to grow or get rid of it?

A You have a member of the nightshade family (*Solanaceae* spp.) sometimes called the mock orange. It does grow very quickly. It has small yellow flowers much like that of a potato or tomato. Its tiny fruit can be poisonous when eaten. Most people choose to get rid of this invasive, potentially hazardous plant using Round-Up spot treatment.

Q Our crape myrtle bush has been well watered and fertilized with a 6-6-6, but it still looks sick. Can you suggest a regime that might put this plant back on track?

A If you are seeing brown-tipped leaves, this indicates water stress. Applying to much of a good thing is often the culprit. Plants receiving too much water can develop an oxygen deficit, also indicated by brown-tipped leaves. Like water, fertilizer can also be over applied. Keep giving your plant good care, but ease back a little.

Q What is the proper treatment for a crape myrtle bush with white spots on its leaves?

A A crape myrtle (*Lagerstroemia indica*) in this condition has powdery mildew. Infected leaves often appear to have been sprinkled with flour. These spots are usually circular and white. With age they begin to look somewhat irregular and darker in color with tiny, black fruiting bodies. The leaves will often become distorted and curled. With a heavy infestation the leaves will die. Spraying with Karathane according to the label directions is the best treatment.

Q How can I help my *ligustrum sinensis* grow faster? Also, what other kinds of hedge plants would you suggest for Southwest Florida?

A The *ligustrum sinensis* should be fertilized on a regular basis. Make sure to give it a good granular fertilizer every three or four months or a good liquid fertilizer, applied lightly, once a month. The pittosporum, dwarf viburnum, and yaupon holly (*Ilex vomitoria*) are all quick-growing hedges that will flourish in South-west Florida.

Q I noticed that the root system of a large ten-gallon azalea appeared to be growing in a circle around the edge of the container. Should this be trimmed when planting?

A Roots that are well overgrown should be trimmed. They are well overgrown if they are coming out of the base of the drainage holes or wrapping tightly around themselves. In general, the root system should be gently opened upon planting to become more accessible to the soil. On the other hand, don't be too quick to trim roots that do not warrant trimming. Be moderate when root pruning and trim only as needed.

Q We are having some building done at our condo, and this requires some shrubs that have been established for fifteen or twenty years to be moved. What is the likelihood they will survive?

A Unfortunately, they will probably not survive. Well-established shrubs can be moved, but this is cost-prohibitive. Paying a knowledgeable person to come out and remove them professionally is costly. It is wiser to buy large shrubs, equal in size, at a local nursery.

Q We have planted some new shrubs near the base of our new home. Unfortunately, more water gets on the windows than the shrubs. What should we do?

A Bubbler type or mist heads on your irrigation system will help keep water closer to the base of the shrubs. A far better idea is to use a soaker hose to put the droplets of water directly at the root system. Not only is this more efficient, providing up to 50 percent more water than overhead irrigation, but it's also a lot easier than cleaning windows.

Q How often should we water established shrubs around the home? This would be ligustrum and viburnum shrubs that are two and three feet tall.

A Shrubs that are fairly well established will not need watering as often as newly planted shrubs. Watering once or twice weekly should be adequate. Often, I will use a moisture meter to determine how moist the soil has become. In general, a slight watering is recommended before applying more moisture. Soggy soil or desert-type soil is not what you want. A happy medium between these two soil types is where shrubs grow best.

Q I have heard that mulching around shrubs can cause trouble? Is this true?

A Yes, it is true. Mulching most plants is a good idea. It helps to conserve moisture, keeps weeds down, and makes a nice, neat appearance. Of course, there is always an exceptions to this rule. Mulch should be kept away from the base of the shrubs. Get the best out of mulching without the side effects.

Q I am ready to plant new shrubs where old shrubs have died out. When is the best time to plant?

A When buying container plants, there isn't really a best time to plant. Most people plant in the spring and fall, partly because winter becomes too cool and summer tends to bring on the doldrums from the heat. When the mood does hit you, realize that the season does not matter all that much. If you plant during the summer months, of course, you will have to water a bit more. With new plants, you should water daily for the first few weeks and then cut back to once or twice a week, depending on the size, type, and variety of plant.

 Should all plants be planted in beds?

Not necessarily. Some plants, such as roses, lend themselves well to bed-type plantings. This is a raised area where the soil can be improved with peat, cow manure, fertilizer, and the like. This may also be said for certain bulbing plants and perennial flowers, such as canna (*Canna* x *generalis*) and calla lilies (*Zantedeschia aethiopica*). For many other shrubs, planting in a site that is improved as needed will give good results.

I purchased a small one-gallon azalea and noticed that it was grown in pure peat. Is there a reason for growing it this way? Should all plants be planted like this?

Azaleas do prefer a peat-type soil, and most nurseries will grow them this way. Azaleas also prefer an acidic soil, which peat is (it's a 4.2 on the pH scale). Many other plants such as ligustrum, viburnum, or hollies (*Ilex* spp.) do just as well in standard nursery soil, although you might notice most bag soils nurseries sell will have a good amount of peat in them. Peat is excellent for holding moisture and nutrients.

Q Our foundation repair workers said that there are cracks in the foundation from plant material such as shrubs or small trees. Is this possible?

A Most of the time when problems with the foundation occur, they are due to sink holes or placing the building in a site that was not appropriate. It is certainly not due to the shrubs, although large trees' roots have been known to crack foundations and should be planted at a distance from a home or condo. This also makes sense where hurricanes and tornadoes are possibilities.

Q Our azaleas are now in bloom, and I was told not to fertilize them at this time. Is this true?

A It is best to use an azalea (*Rhododendron* spp.) fertilizer after the blooming cycle. Truthfully, a light amount of fertilizer even during bloom should not cause any problems. After blooming is also a good time to do some light pruning and reshaping of the azaleas, which will stimulate new growth. This is the beginning phase for the next season's blooms. Remember, azaleas do like a slightly acid soil, so add sulphur.

Q Are there blooming fertilizers for flowers that bloom in early summer, such as the crape myrtle, which flowers every June and then again in August?

A I always recommend fertilizing lightly in the spring as new growth sprouts and again after blooming in June, followed by another application as you put the crape myrtle to bed for winter in September or October. A good fertilization makes for good health, which in turn, assures good blooms for next season.

Q My arborvitae is fifteen feet tall. I want to cut it back but have noticed a browning in the inner portion of the shrub. What should I do?

A The arborvitae (*Thuja* spp.) does need a light trimming on occasion. Major trimming can be a disaster. At this point, you may want to replace the arborvitae with a smaller shrub or do some gradual light trimming on the outer edges. Most of these shrubs look best when allowed to attain their pyramidal shape. When they are boxed or squared off, which is not a normal growing pattern for them, they never look quite as good again.

Q My red-leafed photinia is grouped as a hedge. Unfortunately, they are ten feet tall and rather ugly. Not only are they too thick, but the photinias are also planted where the automatic irrigation system is located. When it rains and then the irrigation system kicks in, they develop a leaf-spotting fungus. Any suggestions?

A Ten feet is quite tall for a hedge planting. Photinias need to be trimmed and kept at about four or five feet to be manageable. If they are ten feet tall, it may be best to simply remove them. As you have discovered, photinia do not like constant irrigation and frequently have problems with fungus. You can treat the leaf-spotting fungus by spraying with a product like Daconil.

Q I have two plantings of Indian hawthorn. In one area they are irrigated every other day, and in the other area they receive very little water. What amazes me is that the one receiving more water looks worse than the one in the dry area. What should I do?

A Like many plants, Indian hawthorns (*Raphiolepis indica*) prefer dry foliage. When constant irrigation is a problem, denuded plants result. Pick the right plant for the right area. One of the best friends of Indian hawthorn has been the forced water restrictions placed on much of Central and South Florida. Before water restrictions became mandatory, a lot of our Indian hawthorns were being killed by over watering.

Q My ligustrum hedge is very thin on the bottom, although it is fairly thick on the top. How can I get it to become thicker near the bottom of the plant?

A Ligustrum hedges do best when trimmed in an inverted V-shape. If ligustrum, viburnum, and many other hedges are allowed to thicken widely on the top, this will shade the middle and lower parts of the hedge, which will not get sufficient sunlight. Proper trimming will solve the problem.

Q I have a number of shrubs that need some minor trimming. Do I have to wait until spring or can this be done at any time of the year?

A Reshaping or light trimming can be done throughout the year on an as-needed basis. This means when there is just a few headers or leaders sprouting out in a certain direction, trim them to keep the shrubs in bounds. This can also be done on most cold-hardy plants in any season.

Q There are some dead twigs in the middle growth of my viburnum. Is there any particular time of the year I should remove this?

A Dead wood can be trimmed out as soon as it is noticed. There is no seasonal requirement. Dead wood is often a harboring place for insects such as borers and other wood-infesting creatures, as well as fungi and bacteria. Quick removal is the best method for dead wood.

Q I have a large agave that recently sent up a flowering spike about twenty feet tall. Is it really true that it takes this plant a century to flower again?

A Although the agave is sometimes called the century plant, this is a misnomer. It does not take a century for this plant to flower. The century plant normally flowers about every ten or fifteen years, afterward sending up many side pups for new generations. The old plant eventually dies within a year or so and, at this point, should be trimmed or dug out. The healthiest pups should be selected to start new plants.

An agave in bloom.

Q My silverthorn is growing as a hedge plant. I grew it because someone told me it makes a nice, thick hedge, which it has. Unfortunately, it is quite difficult to keep it in bounds. Is this typical?

A It sounds like your silverthorn (*Elaeagnus* spp.) is doing its job for you. This plant is fairly difficult to keep in a nice, trim fashion. Hopefully you will receive an electric or gas powered trimmer as a present sometime, because you will be doing a lot of trimming on a regular basis.

5

ANNUALS

Annuals are, technically, plants that grow only one season. But there are many plants that live more than one growing season and are considered annuals because they only bloom once. This often confuses many of us, who are trying to distinguish between annuals and perennials. There are a number of plants that are considered perennials but are truly annuals; for example, the croton (*Codiaeum* spp.), or copper plant, is planted as a shrub. This is especially true when growing in the Tallahassee-Jacksonville-Pensacola area, where the cold often forces perennials to become annuals with seasonal leaf color.

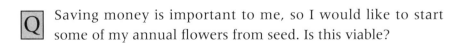

Q Saving money is important to me, so I would like to start some of my annual flowers from seed. Is this viable?

A Yes, there are a number of seed packs available at nurseries. Many annuals can be started from seed. Petunias, pansies (*Viola* x *Wittrockiana*), marigolds (*Tagetes* spp.), zinnias, cockscomb

(*Celosia cristata*), sweet peas (*Lathyrus odoratus*), hollyhocks (*Alcea* spp.), sunflowers (*Helianthus* spp.), morning-glories (*Calystegia* spp.), California poppies (*Eschscholzia californica*), nasturtiums (*Tropaeolum* spp.), moss rose (*Portulaca grandiflora*), and a whole selection of wild flowers are on the list of annual seeds that are grown successfully in Florida.

Q If I want a couple of dozen annuals for a small bed, should I start these from seed or buy them already grown at the nursery?

A This is a difficult question. Obviously, money is saved by growing annuals from seed, but the nurseryman takes the difficult stage of growing healthy plants away from the grower. Some advantages that nurseryman have are controlled soil and controlled conditions. Most nurserymen grow in a peat-perlite, sterile soil. Because of this, they may not experience problems that the average gardener would, problems that can often be frustrating and difficult to resolve. Many of us do get an enjoyment from raising annuals from seed, and this is certainly an option if you're up for the challenge. You can buy a sterilized soil from the nursery as well as viable seed. With a bright sunny spot available and a garden hose nearby, you can be a successful annual grower. For ease and comfort, you can buy them already started in a four- or six-pack, or even gallon-sized containers.

Q I tried to start some seeds I bought from my local nursery in my backyard Florida sand. The results were meager, at best. Do you have any suggestions?

A Our Florida sand does not have enough nutrients or organic matter (less than 1 percent) for healthy plants, and it lacks the appropriate water-holding capacity. Unfortunately, we do have an abundance of nematodes, bacteria, weed seeds, and fungi. I recommend scrapping the idea of planting your seeds in an unprepared soil. Use a sterile potting soil purchased from your local nursery. This can be peat moss, perlite, vermiculite, or washed builder's sand. Establishing soil is like laying the foundation for a house. The house (or plants) will be only as good as the foundation it's set in.

Q I like the idea of having annual flowers, but it seems like a lot of work. Should I consider ground covers or perennials instead?

A Perennials or ground covers could be a better choice for the not-so-avid gardener. Annuals require more work than ground covers or perennials, but the site of a beautiful bed of marigolds (*Tagetes* spp.), petunias, or cockscomb (*Celosia cristata*) is well worth the extra effort.

Q I bought some annuals recently and placed them on my back step for weekend planting. Within a few days, they were dead. What happened?

A More times than not, small, transplanted seedlings are forgotten about and not watered. Remember, in the nursery, they are watered two or three times daily. The best thing to do is to plant your transplants the same day you purchase them. Then begin watering them on a regular basis.

Q I always planted a lot of annual flowers in the springtime up North. Here, I'm confused about what the seasons are in

Florida. My success in planting annuals in July and August is not worth mentioning. Can you help me?

A Seasons are definitely different in Florida. This is even more true when talking about planting annuals. Floridians can grow some of the best spring flowers in the fall. The petunia and pansy (*Viola* x *Wittrockiana*) lead the list for this time of year, along with dianthus, snapdragons (*Antirrhinum* spp.), nasturtiums (*Tropaeolum* spp.), calendulas, flowering cabbage and kale (*Brassica oleracea*), alyssum, and sweet peas (*Lathyrus odoratus*). The fall garden is the best time for annual color.

Q Some of my marigolds have spent seed heads. Is it necessary to take them off?

A As with most other annuals, the removal of the marigold's (*Tagetes* spp.) seed heads is not necessary, although, it is probably good to remove them from an aesthetic point of view. Some people call this dead heading, which means removing the older flowers and an occasional stem that may be sprawling in an odd direction of growth.

Q Many of my annuals fell over at the base. What is causing this?

A This is due to a dampening off disease caused by a number of different fungi, with *Rhizoctonia solani* leading the pack. There is not a successful control for this other than solarizing the soil. Start your plants in a good soilless mix using peat or perlite and spraying with a fungicide as a preventative before the disease raises its ugly head. There are a number of general fungicides available, such as Daconil, Diathane M-45, and others that will do a good job suppressing some of these early fungus problems in annuals.

Q I have quite a bit of Bermuda grass and other weeds growing in a bed that I use for annuals. I have a month before the bed needs to be changed out. What herbicide can I use for these weeds?

A I recommend an herbicide containing glyphosate. This is sold as Round-Up, Kleen-Up, and other trade names. Apply this ten to fourteen days before planting because it will take the herbicide this long to show its effectiveness. It attacks and kills the root system. Be assured that with obnoxious weeds such as sedge (*Carex pendula*), Bermuda grass (*Cynodon Dactylon*), or Torpedo grass, a second treatment will be in order by next season.

Q I live in an upstairs condominium and would like to grow some annuals, but I do not have good growing conditions. Do you have any suggestions?

A Container growing is ideal for your situation. It not only allows you to save space, but it also gives the plants the controlled growing conditions they need. There are many different sizes of containers to choose from, as well as decorative grow boxes. Make sure the container

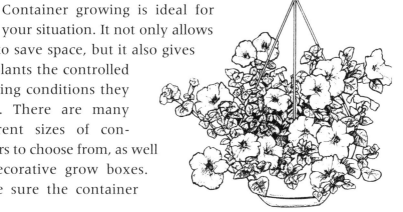

Petunias growing in a hanging basket.

you choose has adequate drainage holes and water a bit more than when growing in the ground. The additional wind factor of being on the second floor may also dry the container plants out more easily.

Q What is the best water-soluble plant food for my annuals?

A There are a number of good water-soluble fertilizers. Peter's, Miracle Gro, Stern's, and Rapid Grow are just a few available products for feeding annuals. You can also consider using Osmacote in addition to other time-released fertilizers that give a longer season for growing annuals. Remember, annuals are heavy feeders. They are started, grow, and die all in one season. This short life cycle makes their nutrition particularly important.

Q I have noticed that some of the annuals I purchased are root-bound. Should I take these apart?

A Absolutely. Annuals get root-bound, which can stunt their growth, and will benefit from you gently pulling or separating the root system. Don't get too carried away with this practice. You should do just enough to stimulate them into their main blooming.

This plant is root-bound.

Q I have seen a tiny plant with white flowers used in a window box. It had a delightful, honey fragrance. Do you know what kind of plant this is?

A This is the annual alyssum. It is sometimes called sweet alyssum because of the sweet, honeylike aroma. It is one of the few fragrant annuals. Alyssum is normally planted in the spring. It can also be planted through summer and in the early fall. It makes an excellent annual, taking the climate and growing conditions well. I haven't detected an insect problem on this plant yet but have experienced an occasional fungus problem. Alyssum makes a great border or window box plant.

Q We have two different types of begonias, and we noticed that the red-colored foliage is better than the all-green variety at taking the Florida sun. Is this correct?

A Yes, the bronze wax-leaf begonia does take the sun better than the all-green-leaved begonia. Even so, make sure to get them in early in the spring, or if you plant them in the fall, cover them at night to protect against freezing. As an early spring or early fall bedding plant, the begonia makes a nice splash of leafy color.

Q I had begonias in the Miami area and kept them alive throughout the winter. Now I'm trying to grow them in the Tampa Bay area, and they die out when frost approaches. Is the growing season that different here?

A Although wax begonias can survive in mild winters in Central and South Florida, the duration of cold and the actual temperature is usually much lower in the Tampa Bay area. There are several different climates throughout Florida. For example, when growing begonias in the Florida Keys, the cold problem is not a factor at all. Many of our more succulent annuals have problems when the temperatures dip down below 32 degrees.

Q I planted some ageratums recently. The nurseryman could not tell me too much about this plant. What can you tell me?

A Ageratums are often used as annuals and are planted in the fall and spring seasons. They have to be protected from cold up North but normally take the cold in Central and South Florida quite well. Ageratums do not seem to have many problems, and they bloom on a constant basis for most of the growing season. This plant should be watered well and then allowed to dry. Using a water-soluble fertilizer or fish emulsion-based fertilizer will produce good results.

Q I used to grow asters in New Jersey. Now that I'm retired and living in Florida, I have not seen any for sale down here. Why is this?

A Asters can be grown here. On occasion, you might find them in four packs in the spring, but normally they have to be grown from seed. Asters are beautiful plants that have temperature, mite, and scale problems, but it is still worth the effort to plant them when they are available.

Q Recently, I saw an annual called the pocketbook plant for sale at my local nursery. What can you tell me about it?

A The pocketbook plant (*Calceolaria* spp.) is also called the slipperwort. This plant comes in a number of different shades that the hybridizers have worked with—often a lemon yellow to a burnt orange flower, which resembles a traditional tan pocketbook. It does well in the fall to winter and early spring garden. They are often used as specimen plants in containers. Treated as an annual, it will do well for short periods of time. It is an interesting addition to any flower bed.

Q We have a partially shaded area where we would like to have some color during the cool season. What should we be looking for?

A Under partially shaded areas, the caladium makes an excellent choice for leaf color. They are normally planted from bulbs in October. Many nurseries will have them available, and they grow well in Florida. Often the bulbs will be set in October and picked up during the wet, summer season due to rotting. Caladiums, sometimes called painted elephant ears, make striking border plants with big green, white, and red variegated leaves.

Q Although my caladiums do not have many problems, I did find a grasshopper eating some of the larger leaves. Is this harmful to the plant?

A The grasshopper you are seeing is called a lubber. They hatch out as small, black grasshoppers with a red stripe and turn into mammoth grasshoppers, growing three to four inches long. When full grown, they are bright yellow with red and black areas. Lubbers are equal opportunity feeders and seem to feed upon a number of large-leafed plants, including caladiums. Spraying with a stomach poison like Sevin or using a contact insecticide such as Dursban will take care of this problem.

Q There is a small, white spath flower growing in the middle of my caladiums. Is this normal?

A This little, spathlike flower is very common. For bulbing plants, use a fertilizer that is higher in potassium and phosphorus, such as a 2-10-10 or 5-10-10. This not only produces a stronger bulb and tuber but also produces the chance of more flowers. Although caladiums are known for their exotic foliage, they do have an interesting spath flower on occasion as well.

Q We recently came across a plant called amaranth globe. What can you tell us about this interesting plant?

A The amaranth globe (*Gomphrena globosa*) does well in full sun and flowers in a range of colors, from (the most common) purple to a reddish-pink to white and even to a soft orange. The plant can grow to twenty inches tall, taking about three months to bloom. The amaranth is planted in spring around March and April, each plant about one foot apart. It is relatively free of problems.

Q In a magazine I saw an annual flower called candytuft. Will this grow in Florida?

A Candytuft (*Iberis umbellata*) is a plant that will grow in full sun in Florida. Normally it is planted either in the fall (early October) or as a spring annual in early March. Candytuft is loved for its colors of white, violet, pink, and red. It is cold hardy here and can grow to twenty inches in height. Since it is a relatively quick bloomer, you can expect blooms in about seventy days. The plant is fairly trouble free, except for an occasional aphid on new growth.

 Can carnations be grown outside as a flowering plant in Florida?

Carnations (*Dianthus Caryophyllus*) remind many of us of high school dances, and they are still used quite a bit today for such occasions. Carnations come in a number of different colors—pink, red, yellow, and white—and can be grown in partial shade to near full sun. They are cold hardy for most parts of Florida, growing to heights of one to three feet. They do have problems with rust, root rot, mites, aphids, and wilt. Even so, they are well worth the battle.

I like the vibrant colors of cockscomb. How can I best blend it in to my Florida landscape?

The cockscomb (*Celosia cristata*) does have extremely vibrant colors for an annual plant. Their unusual colors include a golden yellow, a rich fuschia, a deep purple, and a snowy white. Cockscomb grows in full sun to partial shade. They are tender and should be protected from cold. They grow twenty-four to thirty-six inches tall and bloom in a short period of time, normally sixty to eighty days. Make sure you get varieties or plants in containers that have not been sitting for too long. Ideally, the flower buds are just starting to form. Cockscomb does have occasional problems with caterpillars, but this can be controlled with Sevin, Dipel, or Thuricide.

Can coleus be grown here in Florida?

 Yes, it can. Coleus is a great plant, especially if you enjoy leafy colors. Coleus, with its multicolored leaves, grows in wide ranges of color. Unlike some flowering plants that have a shorter season, coleus tends to give more leafy color for longer periods of time. It is not cold hardy, however, and should be protected to ensure next season's growth.

 Is the African daisy considered an annual or a perennial?

 The African daisy (*Gerbera Jamesonii*) comes in a number of different colors: violet, white, blue, cream, yellow, bronze, and red. They do well in full sun, are cold hardy in Florida, and have relatively few problems. In certain climates, the African daisy is considered a perennial, but when grown in North Florida, it is considered an annual.

 The shasta daisy I have grown has a white flower with a yellow center. Do these flowers come in other colors?

 There are a number of different kinds of daisies with numerous color combinations. The shasta daisy (*Chrysanthemum* x *superbum*), which is a chrysanthemum cross, normally comes as this white flower with the yellow center. They grow well in full sun and are very hardy in Florida. Shasta daisies are planted from August through December about one or two feet apart and reach about the same in height. They take quite some time to bloom from seed, normally about 120 days. This is why most of us buy them already established from the nursery.

Q What type of annual plant can I grow that is unusual and will be a conversation piece?

A I like the Chinese forget-me-not (*Cynoglossum amabile*), which is sometimes planted during the winter season. It will grow in full sun to partial shade. These annuals are planted about eighteen inches apart, taking eighty-five to one hundred days to bloom. They can have some root-rot problems, so plant them in a bed that has not been contaminated before and be sure to use sterile soil when planting.

Q What can you tell me about the gaillardia?

A The gaillardia, or blanket flower, comes in red, orange, yellow, and white. It can be planted just about year round, and the plants should be placed one to one-and-a-half feet apart. The gaillardia will bloom in sixty to seventy-five days. It does best in full sun, reaching heights of eighteen to twenty-four inches. The gaillardia is one of the toughest annuals grown in Florida.

6

PERENNIALS

With the first signs of spring, we are all ready to head back to the garden. And the first thing we want to see is color—and lots of it. The easiest way to add color to your garden is by planting perennials. You can plant them in groupings for waves of flowing color, or you can plant them together with other flowers and shrubs to maintain color over a longer period of time.

There are a few things you need to know about perennials before you get started. First, they have a big problem with weeds. Your best defense against this is to spray the weeds with Round-Up (glyphosate) before you plant flowers. Second, to keep you perennials flowering, pinch off old blooms. This will allow you to enjoy them for much longer. In Florida we also have the advantage of better temperature ranges than most states, allowing us to grow flowers all winter long. Although having year-round gardens does require more attention and care than simple evergreen shrubs, the payoff is beautiful perennials you can enjoy any time of the year.

Q I have heard that there is less work involved in planting perennials than annuals. Is this true?

 A Not exactly. Perennials still require water, fertilization, weeding, mulching, and in many cases, replacement. They also have problems with caterpillars, aphids, canna leaf rollers, and many insects that are host-specific to certain perennials. However, the planting bed does not need to be replaced each time you plant, so this does alleviate some work.

 Q How much fertilizer do we need to apply to our perennials?

 A Some perennials require more fertilization than others. In general, use a good lawn fertilizer, such as a 6-6-6, 8-8-8, or 10-10-10, at a rate of one pound per ten-by-ten area of soil. Some perennials grow best when the soil is improved with extra peat moss, cow manure, and other organic amendments. There are some perennials that do not require a lot of improvement, such as the crinum lily, or the Florida swamp lily. This lily is adaptable to almost any Florida soil. As the name implies, a bit more water will increase its growth. As perennials grow during the season, a water-soluble fertilizer such as Peter's, Rapid Grow, or Miracle Grow can be applied. A blooming-type fertilizer, such as a 5-10-10, can be used for the bulbing or tuberous perennials.

 Q I have a bed of perennial bulbs that includes amaryllis and crinum lilies. Are there any rules on resetting these plants?

A Often when bulbs start setting deeper into the soil, you'll need to replant them. One-third of the bulb should be left above the ground for both amaryllis and crinum lilies. Replanting is a good time to improve the soil. A fertilizer such as a 2-10-10 or 5-10-10 should be used.

Q Quite a few weeds started growing in my perennial bed last season. Are there any weed killers than can safely be used around my beds?

A There are a number of perennial herbicides that you can use. Products containing baylan and dacthal can be effective in stopping the germination of the weed. Often those problem weeds, such as Bermuda (*Cynodon Dactylon*) grass, re-invade the perennial beds. These can be stopped by spot-treating them with an herbicide containing glyphosate, which is sold as Round-Up and Kleen-Up. Remember to apply it just to the weeds, because this is a nonselective herbicide and can kill the perennials as well.

Q Should I mulch the perennial beds around my home?

A Yes. Almost any perennial will benefit from a two- to three-inch layer of mulch. Not only does this help conserve moisture, but it also helps to hold fertilizer and, more importantly, will help to keep weed problems to a minimum.

Q My amaryllis bulbs never seem to have the abundance of blooms they had in their first year's growth, but they have also grown more crowded over the years. What do you suggest?

A Many bulb plants tend to overcrowd themselves. This means you need to separate and replant them. Also, if you have shading problems, a brighter, sunnier location may be in order.

My perennials do well in the full sun, but my garden also has some shady areas. Are there any perennials I can grow in partial shade?

Some perennials that do well in partial shade are the amaryllis, belloperone or shrimp plant (*Justicia Brandegeana*), and caladiums. Carnations (*Dianthus Caryophyllus*), chrysanthemums, coleus, coneflower (*Dracopsis amplexicaulis*), dahlias, daylilies (*Hemerocallis* spp.), ganzanias, society garlic (*Tulbaghia violacea*), larkspur (*Delphinium* spp.), amazon lilies (*Eucharis grandiflora*), calla lily (*Zantedeschia* spp.), blue sage (*Salvia azurea*), shellflower (*Alpinia Zerumbet*), verbena, and even tulips (*Tulipa* spp.) usually grow in a partial shade as well.

How well do tulips grow in Florida?

Tulips (*Tulipa* spp.) are not well adapted to Florida, but they are grown here. They require a certain amount of cool time, and in Florida this normally means placing the bulbs in the refrigerator for about sixty days. You can purchase them in the early fall, chilling them in the vegetable bin of your refrigerator and then setting them out in mid-December or January. They will come up and produce flowers, but the flowers will not last very long. The first warm, winter day will cause them to start dropping their flowers. If you have friends or relatives in the North, you could give them your bulbs after flowering because they will not normally flower for a second year here. In Florida they just don't get the cool time needed to build energy in the leaves, which is necessary for blooming the following season. This is also true for hyacinths (*Hyacinthus* spp.) and narcissus.

Q We are growing asters this year for the first time in our fall garden. They have grown to be about two-and-a-half feet tall, and now they are falling over. Is there anything we can do for them?

A One drawback to growing asters in a fall garden is their tendency to get long and lanky here in Florida. You can buy dowel sticks at most discount nurseries or use small pieces of thin bamboo to tie up the asters. Trimming them back is also an option after flowering. This growing tendency is one reason asters are not a popular perennial here.

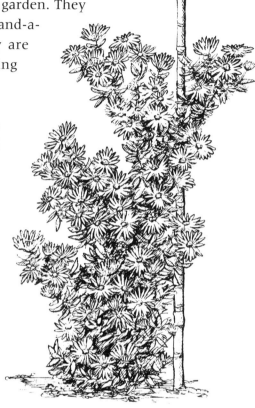

Asters can be staked with bamboo.

Q Carnations have always been one of my favorite perennials, but I have not been successful at growing them in Florida. I have noticed a plant called dianthus, which resembles the carnation and seems to grow well here. Are these two flowers related?

A Carnations, the large ones grown for cut flowers, as well as a number of other cut flowers seem to have problems growing in the Florida heat. It's not that carnations can't be grown here, but they are not that well adapted. Dianthus is a variety of carnation. Also sometimes called "pinks," they do very well here and can last as a perennial. They do have to be cut back a bit for refurbished growth. As a bedding plant and ground cover, dianthus will last a number of years.

✼

Q Our canna lilies look like they have been cut with scissors. What causes this?

A The canna leaf roller loves to attack the canna lily. Spraying with Sevin or an organic material such as Thuricide, also sold as Biotrol/Dipel, should get the problem under control. It is a good idea to use a spreader sticker when applying an insecticide on a shiny-leafed plant such as the canna lily.

✼

Q I was recently given a chrysanthemum plant as a gift, and I would like to plant it in my back yard. Is this possible?

The canna leaf roller causes the plant's leaves to look like they have been cut by scissors.

A Often gift plants have been grown under greenhouse conditions. Although it may never look quite the same as it did when packaged as a gift, you can plant your chrysanthemum in your yard. The chrysanthemum and garden mums in general make good in the Florida fall garden. Plant them in near full sun to partial shade. Chrysanthemums grow best in an improved soil, so add peat moss, cow manure, and 6-6-6 fertilizer. Trimming them back about by about one-half to remove the spent flowers will help initiate new flower buds and make a thicker, bushier flowering plant.

Q My cast-iron plant is growing in a shady spot behind my porch, which is on the north side of my home. It has been doing well there, but recently there is some browning on the edges of the leaves. What is causing this?

A Cast-iron plants (*Aspidistra elatior*) are not very cold hardy and are often injured by cold north winds. This is true even in Florida, at least the north and central parts. Sometimes called the spittoon plant, the cast-iron plant likes a good deal of water. As a ground cover, it can be an easy plant to overlook when watering. So cut back the bad looking leaves, increase the water, and give them a slight fertilization. Even though they will tolerate extreme neglect, cast-iron plants respond noticeably to an increase in care.

Q My neighbor gave me a chrysanthemum plant that is growing tall and leggy. What can I do to restore this plant?

A Often mums are grown in florist-type conditions. They are being produced by hybridizers for slightly different reasons than the average gardener's. Most of the time, these mums can be brought into the garden and grown successfully. To achieve a bushier mum with a more traditional look and flower size, trim them two or three times during the spring and summer.

Q When is the best time to dig up and divide chrysanthemums to get more plants?

 A Chrysanthemums should be dug and divided after blooming. The common flowering time here in Florida is October through December. The mums are triggered into flowering during long-night, short-day periods. After the plants have finished flowering, trim them back, dig them up, and divide them. A number of plants can be had from one chrysanthemum plant.

Q I recently saw a beautiful plant called a columbine in a seed catalog. Can I grow these in Florida?

A Columbines grow well in many cooler parts of the country. Although they have been grown in northern Florida, in the Tallahassee-Pensacola area, most areas of Florida are not cool enough for columbines.

Q I was told that coreopsis is a very attractive plant, but the ones I grow get too tall and fall over. What can I do to make them eye appealing again?

A The coreopsis, or golden wave, is a good-looking plant, but it takes time and patience. Trimming them back constantly can be a fair amount of toil, making this plant somewhat unmanageable for the average perennial grower. If you're up to the task, your hard work will be rewarded with beautiful, bountiful coreopsis.

 Q I miss the crocus we grew in Michigan. Can they be grown here?

A Most of the bulbing plants do not grow well in Florida. If you want to prechill the bulbs and put them out at the end of November or December when cool weather is forthcoming, the crocus could grow for one season. Typically, after that one season, the bulbs would be better off sent back to friends in Michigan.

Q My daylilies are not flowering well. What do you suggest?

A Some of the older varieties of daylilies (*Hemerocallis* spp.) do not grow well in Florida. I recommend visiting your local nursery and buying daylily varieties that are adapted to Florida. These newer varieties will give bigger and better flowers as well as being a welcome addition to any Florida garden.

Q I am looking for a daisy-type flower that grows only thirty inches tall for a border. Do you know of anything like this?

A Consider the African daisy (*Gerbera Jamesonii*). It is a hardy perennial that is often used as a background or dividing plant because of its beautiful flowers.

Q What should I do with my gladiolas after they flower?

A The gladiola (*Gladiolus* x *hortulanus*) grow from corms, a bulblike structure. They should be dug up six weeks after flowering, normally before the foliage turn yellow then brown. The best place to store the corms is in dry peat or sawdust during the

gladiola corm

winter season. Gladiolas can be replanted after the last frost in to the early summer. Some people like to plant them weekly for continuous color.

Q I just came across a flower called blanketflower. It looks pretty rough and tough and might make a welcome addition to the corner of my yard. Can you tell me more about its growing conditions?

A The blanketflower (*Gaillardia* spp.) is similar in appearance to the annual gaillardia. It has hairy, light green foliage and a large, daisylike flower with a reddish center and yellow tinges. It can grow up to thirty inches tall. This hardy plant will grow in almost any Florida soil, and left alone it can spread over a large area in just a few seasons. The blanketflower can be started by seed or by clump divisions from September through January. It is an excellent choice for rock gardens, xeriscapes, and any poor soil areas.

Q I regularly spray my old-fashioned roses, the Maria Louise and the Paul Neyron, with a fungicide. Instead of the blackened leaves turning a nice healthy green, they appear to blacken even more. Can we save them?

A Black spot (fungus), in addition to mildew and spider mites, is a constant problems for roses in Florida. I recommend spraying with a fungicide labeled for black spot. Even with proper applications, it can be persistent, so you may need follow-up applications. If mildew is present, spray with a fungicide called Karathane or a fungicide specifically labeled for powdery mildew. For spider mites, use Kelthane or another insecticide labeled for roses and spider mites.

Q I have a slightly raised mound, almost a small hill, in my yard, which was made by the previous owners. I have tried to plant petunias on the top of it, but they dry out and die. What would grow better in this area?

A You have a number of choices. My favorite is the gazania daisy (*Chrysanthemum* spp.), which displays outstanding color. Gazanias, much like gaillardias and African daisies (*Gerbera Jamesonii*), close their blooms at night. These flowers have a daisy-like bloom that can grow up to three inches across, and they will stay relatively low, growing between sixteen and eighteen inches tall. Gazania would be a good choice for you because they like a moist soil but will tolerate a dry one. Also, they grow in full sun and handle salt well. The easiest way to grow them is already started in containers at the nursery, but you can also start them from divisions. Gazanias make an excellent plant for spring, summer, and early fall bloom.

Q My neighbor has a beautiful daisy collection. She said they were gerbera daisies. Are these a good choice for any Florida yard?

A The gerbera daisies (*Gerbera Jamesonii*), which are native to South Africa, seem to grow well in Florida. They respond well to good care, so do not plant them too deeply and give them adequate moisture as well as occasional fertilizer. For cut flowers, bedding, and border plants, the gerbera is one of the hardiest perennials that gives us one of the widest ranges of color combinations within the same bed. One of the new varieties, called Happy Pot, has an especially large flower and gives us alternate shades of colors, which adds so much beauty to the flower garden.

Q Recently I came across a flowering perennial that was about three feet tall with beautiful blue and purple flowers. Can you tell me what this is?

A This is the lisianthus. It is one of the taller perennials, ranging anywhere from eighteen inches to three feet in height. The white lisianthus are normally the smaller ones, and the pink-blue-purple ones tend to be the largest. They seem to do well in a Florida soil that is not overly wet. Lisianthus flowers during most of the warm months and experiences few insect problems, but it does occasionally develop fungus problems at the base.

Q I've been looking for a small window box plant with a pleasant fragrance. I saw a white one called sweet alyssum. Are there other types of alyssum besides the white variety?

A Sweet alyssum has a wonderful fragrance similar to honey. It can be found in various shades of purple from violet to lilac in addition to white. Sweet alyssum can be used in rock gardens, window boxes, and even as a ground cover. They are normally planted from September through January and bloom in October through June. Under the right conditions, alyssum can grow as a perennial. It can become scraggly and needs trimming back. Be careful not to overwater it.

 Do you recommend verbena as a border plant?

 Verbenas grow low, normally reaching only six to eight inches, making them a good choice for your border. These hardy perennials prefer moist soil and take full sun to partial shade. Plants are normally started from seed or by cuttings. Verbenas are planted anywhere between August and December for a January through July bloom. Occasionally, they have problems with leaf hoppers and spider mites, which can be controlled by spraying with a general insecticide for the leaf hopper and a miticide for the spider mites.

 What are the best types of ferns to plant in the landscape?

 Ferns are often thought of as indoor or porch or patio plants. But in reality, there are a number of ferns that can be used in the landscape. The most commonly grown fern is the Boston fern (*Nephrolepis exaltata* cv. 'Bostoniensis') and offshoots of this variety. But you can also plant holly ferns (*Polystichum Lonchitis*) in the Florida landscape as well as the rabbit's foot fern (*Polypodium aureum*), with staked varieties that cling to trees and boards, and the leatherleaf fern (*Rumohra adiantiformis*), which can be used as a bedding plant.

Q My neighbor has a lily-of-the-Nile that tends to creep over into my yard. Can this plant be cut back without harming it?

A The lily-of-the-Nile (*Agapanthus africanus*) normally grows well in Florida with the exception of North Florida, where it will be injured. Because of its tenacity, the lily-of-the-Nile may need to be cut back at times. Also, the bulblike structure will need to be reset in a new area after a number of years. When resetting, add more organic matter and give a bloomer or bulb-type fertilizer.

Q I was recently given a rose bush. What is the best location for growing roses?

A Roses, like many flowering plants, bloom their best in an eastern setting. The early morning light helps dry off the foliage, which cuts back on the powdery mildew and black spot problems that plague roses. Roses also do best in a good drainage area, so avoid those areas where water tends to stand. People often choose to build beds for their roses so they can dedicate more care to them. You should care for your roses by spraying every few weeks for fungus and insects, and they do require more fertilization than most other perennials.

Q My roses always have black spots with yellow halos around them. Is this the black spot fungus I am always hearing about?

A Yes, this is classic black spot fungus. This fungus disease is the worst problem for roses. Spraying with a good rose fungicide, such as Funginex or Daconil, or a combination of materials, such as Captan or Diathane M-45, every two weeks is the best preventative. Some varieties seem to be even more susceptible to black spot fungus than others. Removing the infected leaves is an important part of good maintenance. You should do this on a daily basis and get rid of the leaves in the garbage.

 I noticed miniature roses at my nursery. Are these easier to care for than larger roses?

 Growing miniature roses has become popular in Florida. They may be somewhat easier to care for than their larger cousins, but only in that they are smaller and require smaller amounts of fertilizer and require less coverage when spraying for a fungus. They will still experience the same problems of the larger varieties. The size is an extra bonus for those who have smaller areas to work with such as in condominiums and apartments.

Q When should I trim my roses?

A Roses can be trimmed at any time during the dormant season, although this varies throughout Florida. Mid-December, January, and February are typically the months to prune roses. Trimming is usually done back to a five leaflet. This means about one-third to a maximum of one-half of the cane is trimmed off. This is especially true of the hybrid tea roses, but you should not be so severe on florabundas, and of course, the miniatures may only be cut a few inches. Be sure to make clean cuts, and when doing specific cuts, be sure to pick the bud, usually one-eighth of an inch above another bud, in the direction in which you want the plant to break or branch out.

Q I have grown climbing roses for about a year. They do not bloom as well as I had hoped they would. Do you have any suggestions?

A Climbing roses do not need to be trimmed as much as other varieties, such as the hybrid teas or florabundas. As their name indicates, they need to climb, so if they are constantly being trimmed back, they will not flower as they should. Climbers are hardier and do not seem to be affected by disease nearly as often as other varieties. One variety, the Don Juan, may last ten to fifteen years with good flowering and requires little care. Fertilize with a good rose fertilizer, lightly, once a month during the growing season.

7

VEGETABLES

Florida is blessed with a climate that can grow veggies year-round. Although we often think of gardening in the spring, many plants can be grown successfully, if not better, in a fall garden. Tomatoes, peppers, eggplants, radishes, broccoli, and onions are just some of the tasty treats you can grow in the fall. Our spring gardens can also contain these vegetables, which extends the season of many of them considerably. Even during the hot, humid summer, our vegetable gardens can produce favorites like collard greens and tomatoes.

There are many reasons people choose to grow their own vegetables. The first is quality; everyone knows exactly what was applied to their veggies and the growing conditions. The second reason is taste, which is of the utmost importance; a ripe, juicy tomato fresh off the vine tastes much better than those bought from the supermarket. Nutrition is another reason people like to grow their own vegetables. Because they are controlling the growing conditions, they are increasing their veggies' nutritional value by amending and fertilizing the soil. And of course, cost is also a good reason to grow your own vegetables. If you are a bottom-line person, you can get a seven- to ten-dollar return for every dollar you put into your vegetable garden. But the best reason of all for growing a vegetable garden in Florida is the fresh air and exercise. Many people enjoy gardening because it relaxes them and takes them back to nature. That's why it's America's number-one pastime.

 My children are interested in starting their own vegetable garden. What would be easiest for them to grow?

 There are a number of easy veggies that are great for children. Radish (*Raphanus sativus*) is at the top of the list because they will start to come up in a short period of time—within three weeks. Leaf lettuce (*Lactuca* spp.), beans (*Phaseolus* spp.), cucumbers (*Cucumus sativus*), peppers (*Capsicum* spp.), and okra (*Abelmoschus esculentus*) are all easy-to-grow vegetables. Of course, this is not the end of the list. Sometimes it is wise to find out the child's favorite vegetable and plant that.

 My garden area has become imbedded in shade. What should I do to grow vegetables in this area?

 Deeply shaded areas can produce the leafy vegetables, such as leaf lettuce (*Lactuca* spp.), mustard and collard greens (*Brassica* spp.), cabbage (*B. oleracea*, Capitata Group), and maybe even broccoli (*B. o.,* Botrytis Group) and Brussels sprouts (*B. o.,* Gemmifera Group).

How important is it to improve the organic matter in my garden soil?

 It is extremely important. The ideal soil will contain 25 percent organic, 25 percent mineral, 25 percent water, and 25 percent air. To attain these ratios in the typical Florida sand, you have to add quite a bit of organic matter. You can do this in a number of ways. You may improve your soil with peat moss, cow manure, leaves, or grass clippings. Or you may garden the Mr. Green-thumb way and use all of the above. In a traditional garden, the soil is tilled to a depth of six inches. After checking the soil's pH, add lime or sulfur and till them into the soil. Many of these amendments do not move through the soil effectively if not mechanically tilled. When growing in containers or earthboxes, you may find that a good potting soil bought in bags is adequate. There are special mixes available for earthboxes, such as Faffard's potting soil, which is a bit on the expensive side but is relatively sterile and will start the veggies off well.

 I noticed recommended planting dates on some seed packets. Should I follow these recommendations?

 These recommendations are helpful for putting you into the right season for that particular vegetable.

 I'd like to have a few vegetables in my mini-greenhouse during the cool season. Do you have any suggestions?

 It depends on the size of your greenhouse and how warm it gets. Vegetables that can be kept all winter long in a greenhouse include the more sensitive ones such as tomatoes (*Lycopersicon* spp.) and peppers (*Capsicum* spp.). Leaf lettuce (*Lactuca* spp.), radishes (*Raphanus sativus*), and onions (*Allium* spp.) do well in moderately cool temperatures.

Q We live in a condominium and have limited space for growing, but we would like to grow a few vegetables. What do you recommend?

A You can enjoy growing vegetables even with limited growing space. A six-inch basket of tomatoes in varieties such as the sugar lump and pixie planted along with miniature cucumbers (*Cucumus sativus*) make a delightful garden. You could even grow leaf lettuce in a small growing box.

Q Is it important to check the pH of the soil in a vegetable garden?

A Yes, it's very important. After checking the pH of the soil, you'll need to take the corrective measures necessary to achieve the proper balance for your vegetable choice. A pH of 5.5 to

Tomatoes grow well in baskets.

6.5 is the norm for vegetables. In a ten-by-ten foot area, add twenty-five pounds of peat moss, twenty-five pounds of cow manure, and some colloidal phosphate along with three pounds of super phosphate and three pounds of a quality fertilizer. Afterwards, till the soil to a depth of six inches. This should get your vegetables off to a good start.

 Years ago I used a material called Vapam to rid my garden of nematodes, but my nurseryman recently said this material has been taken off the market. Why is this?

A Vapam and other chemical materials have been taken off the market for safety reasons. A few methods have been found helpful in keeping nematode populations down. One is to increase the organic matter in the soil, which improves the "good" bacteria that feed upon nematodes. You can also try soil sterilization, solarization. This is done by applying a sheer sheet of plastic over the garden area and putting water underneath it. Place bricks on the ends of the plastic to hold the water in. This method seems to help somewhat and is certainly a thrifty way to keep nematodes down to a minimum.

Q Should I be mulching my vegetable garden?

A In general, mulching can be used in your garden with good results. However, you need to try to keep the mulch away from the stems of the vegetables. Mulching helps conserve moisture. It also serves to hold fertilizer in the soil, and as mulch starts to break down, as many organic mulches do, it will give food value to the plant.

Q Organic gardening seems to be a popular trend these days. Can you tell me more about it?

 A Organic gardening involves growing vegetables without using any chemically derived insecticides or fertilizers. It does require more work and dedication, but the avid gardener can do it quite well. There are pesticides that are environmentally safe, such as Dipel, Thuricide, Biotrol, and Pyrethrene. All of these products contain natural insect killers. For example, Pyrethrene is found in the foliage of chrysanthemums; it gives them a distinctive ability to kill insects. There are also manmade, synthetic pyrethrenes. Organic gardeners will also try to improve the soil by adding compost made from grass clippings, potato peels, coffee grounds, wood ash, leaves, twigs, and similar everyday refuse. Adding manures such as cow or sheep manure is also certainly a good soil builder.

 Q Can I save some of the seeds from my vegetables to plant in next year's garden?

 A This will depend on the variety and whether it was a hybrid plant. If these are hybrid seeds, the plant will not be true. Nonhybrid plants' seeds can be planted and will more than likely produce a crop close to the one grown the previous season. Obviously one of the biggest expenses in the vegetable garden is buying the seeds. Even though the package seems cheap, most packaged seeds today are well over a dollar a package, and each package has very few seeds in it.

 Q Is it better to buy a four pack of vegetables than to start with seeds?

A It depends on how much of a specific variety you want to grow. Remember, the nurseryman has already gotten the seedling through its most difficult growing period: from seedling to the first few inches of growth. At this young stage, they can easily be attacked by fungi and insects. If you only want a dozen plants or so, it would be easier to buy them in packs from the nursery than to plant seeds. Timing may be your biggest concern when deciding whether to buy packs or seeds. For example, you may decide you want to grow tomatoes a month after the seeds should have been planted. In this case, you'll have to buy the four pack.

Q Should I put some granular fertilizer directly in the row of vegetable seeds I am planting?

A No. Most fertilizers contain a certain amount of salt. Although you could get lucky and not experience a burn problem from the salt, it's best to remove the potential for one. You can fertilizer three or four inches away from the seedlings or give them a water-soluble fertilizer just after they have emerged from the soil. With most water solubles, you will only use two tablespoons per gallon of water, so again, the chance of burn is greatly reduced.

Q I received a pamphlet in the mail about vegetable gardening, and it had an article on thinning vegetables. What does this mean?

A Thinning vegetables is the process of removing small seedlings in order to allow more growing room. Radishes (*Raphanus sativus*), onions (*Allium* spp.), carrots (*Daucus Carota* var. *sativus*), peas (*Pisum* spp.), beans (*Phaseolus* spp.), and even tomatoes (*Lycopersicon* spp.) can be thinned out. Choose the seedlings that are set too close together. This will give the remaining plants the growing room needed to mature and produce the desired vegetables.

Q Last season my lima beans had some spotting on the bottom leaves. First, the leaves would turn yellow, and then the rest of the plant would shut down. What caused this?

A Many beans, especially lima beans (*Phaseolus limensis*) and butter beans (*P. lunatus*), when grown in Florida, are attacked by fungi. This often starts at the base of the plant where the lower leaves are attached. As water and precipitation accumulate, the fungi spores are splashed up onto the leaves. Typically, the bottom part of the plant dies first with the upper part following. It is a good idea to spray with a fungicide such as Diathane M-45, Daconil, or Captan on a preventative basis.

Q My grandfather used to plant all his vegetables on a raised mound. He referred to this as hill gardening. I have not seen this procedure done with vegetables here. Is there any reason?

A Hill, or raised, gardening was once common in wet parts of the country, where water settles in the clay soil. In the Florida sand, and with most of us growing our vegetables in artificial containers or raised beds, mound gardening is not necessary. Strawberry (*Fragaria* spp.) and tomato (*Lycopersicon* spp.) gardeners will still raise their plants up a little if drainage appears to be a problem.

Is there a special fertilizer I should use in my vegetable garden?

 Not really. You can use a number of fertilizers in your vegetable garden. Florida soil is typically lacking in nitrogen and potash, and most fertilizers contain both of these elements. However, you do need to make sure you are adding sufficient phosphorus because you are likely to experience problems if this level gets too low in your soil. Many of our root crops require extra phosphorus, which is represented by the second number on a fertilizer bag. As long as your vegetables are getting nitrogen, phosphorus, and potassium, along with trace elements, such as calcium, manganese, magnesium, iron, and zinc, they should grow well.

Q How often should I fertilize my vegetable garden?

A What type of fertilizer you use will determine how often you use it. If you use a long-lasting fertilizer, such as a 6-6-6 or 8-8-8, fertilizing once a month will be sufficient. But if you are using a water-soluble fertilizer, you will have to apply it at least once a week. For those who want to grow champion vegetables, use a reduced-strength (one-quarter strength) water soluble on a constant feed program.

Q I would love to plant a vegetable garden, but the site I have chosen is plagued with fire ants. What approach could I use to rid my garden site of these pests?

A Diazinon and Dursban can both be used in and around the garden. It is always wise to read and follow label directions. Ant baits can also be used around the perimeter of the garden.

We raised asparagus when we lived in Michigan. Is it possible to grow it here?

Asparagus can grow here, although it is not well adapted to Florida. Growing a five or six-foot ferny plume is easy; the problem will be getting the delicious spears. Plant your asparagus in a bright, sunny spot with plenty of room and where you can easily control the water and add organic matter. If you can keep your asparagus dormant long enough in the spring, you will get the spears.

 When is asparagus harvested?

Most growers recommend allowing asparagus to grow for two years before harvesting. The intention is to allow the asparagus to build more energy into the root system and produce bigger spears, but this doesn't always happen in Florida. I have grown asparagus and harvested the first year with good results.

 Do pole beans grow well in the fall garden?

Pole beans are great for the fall garden, planted in September. As a matter of fact, they do equally well in the spring garden, which is typically planted in March or April.

 I read that vegetables should not be planted before October 1 in Florida. Is this accurate?

A People often fear planting in September because it is considered a hurricane month, but many vegetables can be planted early in this month. Besides, if a hurricane should hit, the last thing I would be concerned about would be losing my early-planted vegetables.

Q Are wax beans easier to grow than pole beans?

A Many beans (*Phaseolus* spp.), including wax beans, green beans, and some of the bush beans, seem easier to grow in Florida than pole beans. But pole beans are actually very easily grown—they just need a structure to grow on.

Q When I leave my pole beans on the main stalk too long, they tend to stop producing. Is there a general rule on when to harvest?

A Pick early and often is the general rule when harvesting pole beans. You want to keep the beans from aging. Once they have swelled and developed in the pod, they have grown too long.

Q I have had four good pickings off of my pole beans, but now the plant has withered and stopped producing. Is this normal?

A Four or five pickings is an exceptional crop for pole beans. If it is early enough in the season, you might want to thin out some of the beans that have done well and start new plants.

Q My pole beans have a mite problem. Do these normally attack beans?

A Mites can attack many plants, beans (*Phaseolus* spp.) included. If your beans are under attack, spray with Kelthane according to label directions. You can also use one of the insecticides labeled for spider mites on vegetables.

Q Caterpillars are curling up on the edges of my pole bean leaves. What should I do?

A There are a number of successful kill treatments for the caterpillar. Dipel or Thuricide can be used, as well as liquid or dusting Sevin. Organic growers can use an organic powder and should have good success. Caterpillar attacks can cause a severe breakdown of pole bean production if not brought under control.

Q Can I grow Brussels sprouts in Florida?

A Brussels sprouts are easy to grow as long as you know the season for them—timing is essential. October, November, and December are excellent months for planting Brussels sprouts for the winter garden, and February and March for the spring garden.

Q I love to grow cabbage in my garden, but it always splits in the center. What can I do to prevent this problem?

A As with most of our leafy vegetables, harvest early, especially if weather conditions are still hot and dry. Make sure your cabbage (*Brassica oleracea*, Capitata Group) receives plenty of water, which is crucial to leafy vegetables.

Q When I grew carrots in Pennsylvania, they grew beautifully, but in Florida my carrots look deformed and discolored. What's happening?

A Florida-grown carrots (*Daucus Carota* var. *sativus*) do sometimes suffer from foliage diseases as well as nematodes. The ideal planting area for carrots is a raised bed or earthbox with a well-prepared soil such as a loose, sandy loam. Thinning out small carrots will allow the remaining plants to grow larger and longer. And of course, be sure to water well.

Q Our carrots are woody and pithy. What can I do to make them sweet?

A Florida's hot temperatures can be a strain for carrot growth. It is important to plant them early. Also, water is the key for sweet carrots. You should water every day at first growth and then gradually cut back to three or four of times a week, depending on rainfall.

Q I planted corn with three feet between each plant, but the ears I got were not filled out well. What should I do to get full ears of corn?

A Corn (*Zea Mays*) should be grown in a rich soil with moderate, continuous moisture and heavy fertilization. Since it is a grass member and wind pollinated, planting in a series of two or three parallel rows is important to ensure pollination.

Does corn fair well in the cool season?

 The best planting times for corn are mid-September and early spring. A freeze can be a problem for winter corn, and you'll have to keep an eye out for the earworm in the summer months.

 I found tiny worms feasting on the ends of the ears of my corn. What are these little creature and how do I get rid of them?

 This is the corn earworm. It has ruined more ears of corn than almost any other critter. Some growers will put a drop or two of mineral oil on the flower silks as they start to tassel. The idea is that the butterfly will not be able to lay eggs on the tassels effectively. Also, spraying with traditional insecticides has had some degree of success.

 What varieties of corn grow best in Florida?

 There are a number of varieties that grow well here. The Silver Queen (a white corn), Gold Cup, Golden Security, and Seneca Chief are just a few. Corn takes between eighty and eighty-five days from planting to harvest, so get your corn in early.

 My cucumbers have white spots on their leaves. Is this a bug?

If the white spots are powdery, it is probably powdery mildew, which is a fungus disease. Spray with a fungicide that is labeled for cucumbers (*Cucumis sativus*) and powdery mildew.

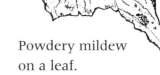

Powdery mildew on a leaf.

 I am raising cucumbers for the first time and find harvesting a bit of a challenge. Are there any signs I should look for?

Like many vegetables, cucumbers shouldn't be left to grow too large on the plant. This causes the plant to shut down production too soon. Harvesting is best done when the cucumbers are two-thirds their normal size. Use the ones you see in the supermarket as a guide.

 I planted a dwarf variety of cucumber that did not grow well for me this season. What did I do wrong?

Sometimes the smaller cucumbers will grow well, but they don't produce like the larger ones. Not only do the smaller ones produce small fruit, but they are also prone to insects and diseases, which limits their production. Try planting a larger variety such as Poinsett or Ashley.

 My one little cucumber plant is not flowering. What can I do to help it spring into action?

Without pollination, production does not occur. No flowers, no fruit. You might want to use a bloomer-type fertilizer, which is higher in phosphorus and potassium, such as a 2-10-10 or 5-10-10.

Q The cucumbers growing in my garden are getting little wormholes in the fruit. This is particularly annoying because the fruit appears healthy until harvest. What can be done to prevent this?

A The old standbys Dipel and Thuricide will help you get rid of these worms.

Q I am growing some pretty bitter cucumbers. How can I improve their taste?

A When the heat in Florida is excessive, cucumbers often over-ripen with a yellowing on the outer skin instead of their typical dark green color. Make sure to keep the moisture level up and plant them in an early fall or early spring garden. This will help, but if the temperatures get too hot, you will still end up with the bitter cucumbers.

Q Years ago when I tried to grow cucumbers they were either pulpy or had scabs on the outer skin. What do you recommend for the Florida garden?

A Cucumbers have improved in their growth habits over the last twenty years or so. There are new varieties grown for best production as well as ones that do not produce the indigestion problems of the older varieties. Try the cucumbers such as the Poinsett, Ashley, Pixie (picklers), and even the burbless varieties.

Should I mulch around my cucumbers?

 Mulching is important around cucumbers. The cucumbers usually grow near the soil's surface, an area where mildew and rots occur. By having a layer of fresh mulch underneath the fruit, the chances of these problems are lowered. Also, mulch will help regulate moisture and cut out one of the biggest chores in gardening: weeding.

 I read about the cucumber beetle in a magazine. If these become a problem, should I treat them with Rotenone?

 The cucumber beetle, and a couple of other beetle varieties that bother the cucumber in Florida, can be controlled in many cases simply by picking them off the plant. Rotenone can be used, and many organic groups consider this a safe material. Always read and follow label directions, of course. You may have to call a couple of nurseries or garden supply stores to find this particular product.

 When should I plant my bulbing onions?

 Bulbing onions (*Allium* spp.) should be planted in the fall (October and November) and can be planted until spring (March and April).

 My bulbing onions are about two or three inches in diameter. Is it time to harvest?

A When one-half to three-fourths of the tops have fallen over, dig the bulbs up and let them dry out for a couple of days. Do not water for two days before you harvest. If it rains, allow the onions to dry in the garage or another dry area. Store them in a cool, dry place.

Q When I am using onion transplants, how deeply should I plant them?

A You don't need to plant them too deeply; one-quarter to one-half inch should be sufficient. If some fall over, don't worry—this often happens. Just replant them

Q What varieties of onions perform best in Florida?

A There are many varieties from across the country that do well here. A few you might want to try include the Texas Grano, Excel, and Granex.

Q We would like to grow multiplying onions so we can have them over longer periods of time. How do they normally arrive?

A Onions can be started from seeds, bulbs, or trays and packages from the nursery. Multipliers will never bulb, but they will give more of the same onion, just as the name implies. Bulbs are preferred for quick eating, but some people prefer to buy the ones already started in packages from the nursery. Green onions, from bulbs, are available anytime at local nurseries.

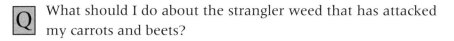 What should I do about the strangler weed that has attacked my carrots and beets?

This killer is the dodder strangler. It can be a major problem, especially for citrus growers. The dodder looks like a yellow to green string that attaches itself to plants and chokes the life out of them. Unfortunately, there is no spray for this strangler so you'll have to physically cut it out from the root.

I'd like to grow broccoli in my vegetable garden. Is this possible in Florida?

Broccoli (*Brassica oleracea*, Botrytis Group) is one of the easiest vegetables to grow, both in the fall and spring garden. Scientists have found that broccoli, along with its relatives Brussels sprouts and cabbage, reduces the risk of certain types of cancer besides being beneficial to overall good health.

My broccoli is turning into a yellow bouquet quickly. What have I done wrong?

Broccoli requires a good deal of water and cooler temperatures. Often in Florida, cool weather is followed closely by warming trends, and broccoli does not respond well to this turn of events. This weather pattern is also a problem when growing some of the leaf vegetables.

Q When growing broccoli, is it better to start with seed or from transplants?

A I have grown broccoli by both methods and prefer the ease of broccoli from plants that have already been started. The most difficult part of the garden chore has been done for you, giving you more time to plant other veggies.

Q How well do Brussels sprouts grow here?

A These tiny cabbages grow well during the cool season. As the heads begin to get crowded, break off the lower leaves to allow more growing room

Q I have a caterpillar curling up in the new tender leaves of my Brussels sprouts. How do I get rid of him?

A Use Sevin, liquid or dust, or an organic insecticide, such as Dipel or Thuricide, which contains *bacillus thuringiensis*. This will do a good job on many of the looper caterpillars, which is what you have, not only on Brussels sprouts but also on broccoli and cabbage.

Q I noticed tiny green dots on my new cabbage leaves. What is this?

A These are aphids, and they love to attack new growth on cabbage, broccoli, and Brussels sprouts. Spraying with an insecticide such as Sevin, Diazinon, Malathion, or Dursban, according to label directions, should help. There are also organic pesticides available for aphid control or you can spray a soapy water solution.

Q My Brussels sprouts take a long time to sprout. Is there anything I can do to make them sprout sooner?

A Make sure to set your Brussels sprouts out as early as possible in the fall and water them well. A bloomer-type fertilizer, such as a 5-10-10 or a 10-10-10 seems to help Brussels sprouts flourish in production.

Q If I use Dipel or Thuricide, how soon can I harvest my cabbage afterward?

A One advantage of using an organic pesticide such as these is that harvesting can be done the same day as the application.

Q There are tiny worms eating on the small cauliflower heads in my garden. What should I do?

A Worms enjoy cauliflower (*Brassica oleracea*, Botrytis Group) as much as we do. As with other members of this family, spraying with Thuricide or Biotrol should help keep the caterpillars under control.

Q I tried growing cauliflower in the early summer last year, but it did not grow well. What did I do wrong?

A Cauliflower is a cool-season vegetable. They are in the same group (*Brassica oleracea*) as broccoli, Brussels sprouts, and cabbage. You should plant your cauliflower in October and be sure to keep them moist—don't let them dry out.

 Is there a best planting time for lettuce?

 Typically head lettuce (*Lactuca* spp.) needs to be planted in the cool season. If you want to grow lettuce during the warm season, try the leaf lettuce. It will take the heat better if harvested early. Once flower heads start on lettuce, it has bolted and the flavor will be bitter.

 Will head lettuce grow in Florida?

 For the average grower, leafy type lettuce has proven more successful than head lettuce. However, if head lettuce is planted in the early fall garden, harvested early, and watered on a regular basis, it can form great heads.

My lettuce tends to be bitter. Is there something I can do to improve its flavor?

One of the best things to do is get a jump on the gardening season. Lettuce should be planted when it is still cool; in fact, a frost is a better risk factor than extreme heat. Also, make sure water is regularly applied. Be sure to harvest early to ensure sweet, tasty lettuce.

Q I have heard that leaf lettuce can extend my garden for quite some time. Why is this?

A Leaf lettuce can be harvested by picking off individual leaves. People usually do this when they need only a small quantity. This will encourage more leaves to grow, giving you lettuce over a longer period of time.

Q When I planted watermelons last season, they not only grew in the garden but took over part of my lawn. Is this normal?

A This is one of the major reasons most people choose not to plant watermelons (*Citrullus lanatus*), as well a squash (*Cucurbita* spp.) and pumpkins (*Cucurbita* spp.). These vegetables tend to take up a great deal of garden area. In fact, it is not unusual for them to cover a ten-by-ten foot area. But if you really love watermelon, the taste of a fresh, juicy one will be the reward for the extra growing space needed.

Q What varieties of watermelon are recommended for the Florida garden?

A For the larger types, the Charleston gray, Congo, and jubilee are recommended, and for the smaller varieties, you can choose between the New Hampshire midget or the sugar baby.

Q When should watermelons be put into the garden?

A Typically watermelons should be planted in the spring garden, around March. They will take approximately eighty to one hundred days from the time that you set them until the time of harvest. A weekly spray program is advisable to control fungus diseases when growing watermelons.

 How do I know when my sugar baby watermelon is ripe?

 Just because a sugar baby watermelon is smaller doesn't mean that it doesn't fit the same rules as harvesting for the larger varieties. Normally the side that the watermelon is sitting on will be a creamy, yellow color. Also, when you thump the watermelon with your finger, you will hear a thud that indicates a thick, full watermelon.

 My okra have aphids and ants crawling on them. Why is this vegetable being attacked by both insects?

Aphids and ants are mutually beneficial insects. The ant feeds on the secretion that the aphid leaves behind after it sucks on the plant's tender growth. The aphids are helped out by the ants who pick them up and carry them to new places on the plant.

I tried growing kale in my garden for the first time this year, but it's turning out rather tough. What do you suggest I do?

Kale is an attractive green, but it can become tough when allowed to grow too large. Pick the leaves when they are young and tender. Kale can be used as a garnish around plates because it doesn't wilt quickly, but it is also highly nutritious and is used as a cooking green.

Q One of my gardening friends told me to start my eggplants from those already started at the nursery. Is this what you recommend?

A Eggplants are sensitive to cold, so most gardeners like to purchase their plants already started in order to get fruit before the cold snap occurs.

Q What variety of eggplant should I grow and how much space will it need?

A One variety I recommend is the Florida market. It seems to be more well adapted to our growing conditions. You may find other varieties grown in your local nurseries that are suitable as well. As a general rule, give them at least three feet between rows and about the same between each plant. If you plant them much closer, competition from roots and shading can interfere with the ultimate production.

Q Can you give me more information on growing English peas in Florida?

A English peas (*Pisum sativum*) prefer the cool season. Planting at the end of October or in early November helps English peas thrive. Add extra peat and cow manure to your soil because peas prefer an improved soil along with adequate moisture. When planting, leave thirty to thirty-six inches between plants; they will begin to produce in about fifty days. English peas can experience problems with fungus on the leaves, which will cause the plant to shut down early.

125

Q My green peppers are turning yellow and red, and I noticed that the plant quit producing at this point. Is this normal?

A Like most vegetables, preventing green peppers (*Capsicum* spp.) from ripening on the plant will improve production. Harvest early, but make sure the vegetable is allowed to reach its maximum size.

Q Is it normal for a pepper plant to last a number of years?

A It is not uncommon for the pepper to overwinter here, making this annual plant a perennial. I have had pepper plants the last three or four years, but the peppers almost always tend to grow smaller. Nevertheless, it is quite a novelty, and if you just want a few peppers to chop into a salad, size doesn't matter.

Q My green peppers did not get as full this year as they should have. Do you know what might have happened?

A Peppers, like most vegetables, prefer a pH of 5.5 to 6.5, which is slightly acid. So check the pH of your garden soil to make sure it is in a good growing range. If you find that it is too acidic (this is a rarity in Florida), add lime to the soil. Green peppers need a steady supply of water; if allowed to get too dry, they will often get a bit stunted. Also, peppers are heavy feeders and need to be fed lightly, about once a week, with one-quarter strength of a water-soluble fertilizer.

Q Do you recommend planting potatoes that have started eyes?

 A Absolutely. Some Florida varieties of potatoes (*Solanum tuberosum*) to grow are the red Pontiac, sebago, kennebec, and the red lasoda. All you need is a good couple of eyes and a fairly large chunk of potato.

Q When do I harvest my potatoes in Florida?

A Harvest potatoes when they have started to flower or when they have been there the required length of time, which is eighty to ninety days. Potatoes will often flower or wilt over, especially when grown at the time of year a frost may occur. New potatoes can be harvested almost anytime during their growing period.

Q What radish varieties are recommended for growth here?

A The cherry belle, comet, early scarlet, white icicle, and sparkler (a white-tipped variety) are all radish (*Raphinus sativus*) varieties that grow well in Florida.

Q Can radishes be started only from seeds or can I purchase already-established plantings?

A Radishes are almost always found in seed packets. This is because most root crops do not transplant well. I have tried to move a few radishes just to test the results of the move, and when the radishes were young, I had some success. Still, it is not typically recommended.

 We enjoyed growing rhubarb when we lived in the Midwest and would like to try growing it here. Is this a good idea?

 Unfortunately, there are a few vegetables that are not well adapted to Florida, and rhubarb (*Rheum* spp.) is one of them. I'm not telling you not to try it, but most attempts are futile. The frozen food section of your grocery store or relatives and friends still living in the Midwest may be your best hope of obtaining that delicious flavor you desire.

 Is spinach grown in the Sunshine State?

 Yes, primarily as a cool-season crop. Spinach (*Spinacia oler-acea*) needs to be planted early (late October or early November) in the fall garden. Varieties grown here include the Virginia Savoy, Dixie, or market hybrid 7. It will take forty to forty-five days from planting until harvest.

We would like to plant spinach in our spring garden. Is this possible?

A summer spinach, such as New Zealand spinach, will take the heat much better than other varieties and is similar in taste to the cool-season spinach. It is normally planted in March or early April and is harvested in about sixty days.

Q Pumpkins go hand in hand with Halloween, and I would like to try growing some to be ready for that holiday. Can that be done?

A Yes, pumpkins (*Cucurbita* spp.) can be grown here, although they have their share of problems, such as powdery and downy mildew. You'll want to get a hybrid seed from your local nursery or garden supply store and start them in mid-June or July. This should time out right for that Halloween picking.

Q I know there are different types of squash. What are the best ones for Florida?

A The winter squash (*Cucurbita* spp.) takes almost twice as long to grow as the summer squash, but it also has a harder outer shell that allows it to last longer on the vine. Some early summer squashes you can plant are the early prolific, straight or crook neck, zucchini, or patty pan. Winter squashes include the table queen, butternut, and alagold. Both the summer and winter squash are planted in spring (February and March).

Q My zucchini squash always gets this white powder on it and shrivels and dies long before I can harvest the first fruit. What can I do to prevent this?

A No doubt this is powdery mildew. I recommend spraying with a fungicide long before you see the first sign of it. You can use Captan, Diathane M-45, or another fungicide labeled for vegetables.

Q My squash grow well and flower abundantly, but very few of the flowers actually set fruit. Why is this?

A Typically when squash first starts to flower there is an abundance of male and female blooms. Of course, these have to be pollinated from one to the other in order for fruit to set. You might not have enough pollinators—bees, butterflies, etc.—in your area. If this is the problem, you can actually pollinate the blooms yourself by touching one flower to the other.

Q My squash all seem to start rotting where they touch the ground. What can I do to prevent this?

A One trick is to place a small piece of wood underneath the squash. Fresh, uncontaminated straw also makes a good bed. This prevents a disease from occurring in the layer of squash that touches the ground. Also, spray with a fungicide on a preventative basis.

Q There is a mottled, green-yellow look to my yellow squash. Is this dangerous?

A This pattern is caused by the mosaic virus. Although its outer appearance looks unappetizing, it does not actually harm you to eat the fruit. There is no known control for this virus, so at the end of the season, discard the plants and try to control insects such as squash bugs and aphids, which are most likely the spreaders of this viral disease.

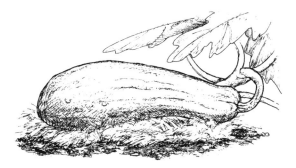

To prevent disease, place a layer of hay under
your squash so it doesn't touch the ground.

 I have heard that sweet potatoes grow well here. Is this true?

 Sweet potatoes (*Ipomoea Batatas*) will indeed grow like weeds
in Florida. As you may know, sweet potatoes need a long
season, often 140 to 160 days, possibly even more. Florida's long
warm season is ideal for growing sweet potatoes.

 One of my friends grows sweet potatoes as his ground cover.
Is this common in Florida?

 It's not common, but it is a great idea. The heart-shaped leaf
of the sweet potato is attractive, resembling the leaf of its
third cousin, the morning glory. And sweet potatoes give you the
benefit of vitamins and minerals. One study reported that sweet
potatoes give you more important vitamins and minerals than any
other vegetable.

 I have been growing my sweet potatoes all summer long and
into the fall. Now, in December, an early frost has occurred.
Will this hurt my sweet potatoes?

A This is the perfect time to harvest them. There should be an ample supply of sweet potatoes underneath the vining growth you have been cultivating for such a long time. Sweet potatoes, in Florida, often get frozen back but will come out with new growth. So more sweet potatoes can be harvested in the same area next year as long as any part of the sweet potato or stem is left growing.

Q Is there a special fertilizer I should use on my sweet potatoes?

A Sweet potatoes are soil tolerant and do not require a lot of fertilization. I would use a 5-10-10 fertilizer, which is lower in nitrogen and higher in phosphorus and potassium, on most rooting crops.

Q Can strawberries be grown in Florida?

A Strawberries (*Fragaria* spp.) are a favorite in Florida. In fact, every year there is a strawberry festival in Plant City, where strawberry is an important crop.

Q What varieties of strawberries do you recommended for growth in Florida?

A The most commonly grown right now are the Florida 90, tioga, and Sequoia, but each year new varieties are developed in nurseries. Strawberries are grown bare root or in small containers that are set out in the fall and harvested in the spring.

They are treated as an annual here, although they have the potential to last more than one season.

 I sometimes see strawberries planted on raised mounds. What is the reason for this?

Good drainage is important for strawberries, and planting them on a mound helps this. Plastic is often used underneath the strawberries to cut down on soil-born disease as well as watering problems.

The tomatoes in my fall garden grow well and appear to be healthy, but then they freeze before any real production occurs. What should I do?

The smaller varieties of tomatoes (*Lycopersicon* spp.), such as cherry, sugar lump, and Roma, are best grown when the weather starts to turn cold. Normally if you are having problems harvesting, this indicates that you are not starting them early enough in the season. Many books recommend putting out tomatoes in October, but try to get them planted by early September in Florida. Even with started plants, they then need between sixty-five and eighty-five days from planting to harvest. This does put Floridians dangerously close to the first freeze, which is around mid-December in most of the state. Obviously, planting is even earlier in Tallahassee and Pensacola than in Central and South Florida. When planting tomatoes in the fall garden, try using a product called Blossom Set. It helps tomatoes set when temperatures are slightly cooler.

Q What are some of the tomato varieties that grow well here?

 A Homestead, Indian River, and Manalucie are larger varieties that will grow well. For smaller varieties, you can choose between the cherry and the sugar lump. Even some of those that were grown up North, such as better boy and big boy, can be grown in Florida. A paste tomato, such as the Roma, is popular here, as is the Tiny Tim, which can be grown in hanging baskets when space is limited.

Q I was at a nursery recently buying some tomato plants, but the ones available were all tall and lanky. Isn't this a bad sign?

A You generally do not want the tall, lanky vegetables because they are too far along. However, this rule does not apply to tomatoes. In fact, tall tomato plants that have been in containers too long often have advantageous roots coming out along the stems. After digging the planting hole slightly deeper than normal, you can sink the tomato stem in, and these rootlets will start growing.

Q I want to grow my tomatoes in large containers. Do tomatoes lend themselves to this?

A Yes, tomatoes can be grown in all types of structures. Almost any variety can be grown in five-gallon containers. You might have to build a structure for it to be staked to, or you can buy a tomato ring at any nursery or garden supply store.

Q Can I start tomatoes from cuttings?

 A Tomatoes often have small suckers that are removed, and these suckers can be used to start new plants. The advantage to using a cutting is that they are already well established and, therefore, will be ready for production sooner.

 Q I saw you on television with a tomato-potato plant. How did you do this?

A Tomatoes and potatoes are in the same family, Solanum, and this makes them potentially graftable. I started a small potato plant, and when it started growing, I grafted a small tomato plant onto it by connecting the cambium layers of each plant. This was really a novelty idea. Often the graft breaks out and really does not produce any kind of fruit.

 Q My tomatoes start to set, but then they get this brown spot on the bottom of the fruit that turns mushy. What's causing this?

A This is called blossom end rot, and it is caused by a lack of calcium. You can purchase a blossom end rot spray at most nurseries. This is a quick-acting source of calcium. When sprayed early enough in the growing season, it will rectify the problem.

Q My tomato plants start with yellow leaves on the bottom of the plant, and then the plant goes from green to yellow to brown and eventually dies. Why is this?

A Tomatoes are susceptible to a number of fungus problems. This is one reason why variety selections are labeled VFN (verticillium, fusarium, and nematode) resistant. A fungicide labeled for vegetables, such as Captan, can be sprayed on a preventative basis.

Q My tomato plants are growing in an area where we sprayed for weeds last year. I noticed that their leaves have curled up tightly. Is this caused by the weed killer?

A Often when a tomato plant's leaves curl up, a weed killer is the cause—especially the 2,4-D type weed killers. Try to keep weed killers far away from tomato plants because they are highly sensitive to them.

Q My tomato plants look wilted in the middle of summer. Is there anything I can do for this?

A Some varieties take the heat better than others. One variety that takes the heat better is called heat wave. Also, the smaller varieties such as the cherry and Roma tolerate the heat well. Our extreme summer heat and humidity can be quite a strain on tomato plants.

tomato horn worm

Q My tomato plant has a large, three-inch worm with a point near the end of its tail. What is it and how do I get rid of it?

A You are describing the tomato horn worm, which is common on tomatoes. It is the larvae stage of the large hawkmoth. Organic gardeners like to physically kill them. You can also spray with Sevin, Dipel, or Thuricide. Unfortunately, this is a problem you just have to deal with when raising tomatoes in the spring and early summer garden.

Q When we get the first freeze in mid-December, can I harvest the green tomatoes and still expect them to ripen?

A Most of the time large fruit on the tomato plant will ripen. You can help them along by placing them in a paper bag with tomatoes that have already started to ripen or placing them in with a piece of apple wrapped in newspaper or paper towels. The gas coming off the apple as it browns causes the tomato to ripen in a day or so. Green tomatoes can also be fried or made into a relish.

Q I noticed in my spring and early summer garden that the tomatoes get cracks on the tops of the fruit. How can I prevent this?

A Try to make sure your tomatoes are watered evenly. Sometimes when we do not water on a regular schedule, the fruits will crack. Also, if the foliage can remain over the fruit, the risks of cracking and sun scald are reduced. Harvesting the tomatoes a few days early will also help.

8

FRUIT

Florida is perhaps the state best known for its tropical fruit paradise. We have an amazing variety of fruit trees, especially in Central Florida and farther south. As we discussed in chapter 2, trees are an investment, and selecting a tree is a decision that should be made seriously. When selecting a fruit tree, you are not only concerned about landscape placement and growth habits but also about bountiful production and sweet-tasting fruit. So besides knowing how much sun a particular plant needs or how tall it will grow, you need to know if its fruit will grow large and tasty in your location.

People often think of citrus when they think of fruit trees in Florida, and citrus is king here for a reason. Our climate is ideal for raising all kinds of citrus; we can grow it in North, Central, and South Florida. Grapefruits, lemons, tangerines, tangelos, kumquats, oranges, and limes are just some of the citrus fruits that flourish in Florida. But these are not the only fruits that thrive here. Avocados, star fruit, mangos, litchis, and other tropical delicacies can be found growing in abundance. With so many tempting choices, deciding which fruit to grow is more of a challenge than growing it.

 I love mangos. Can they be grown in the middle of Florida?

 It really depends on where you live in of the middle of Florida. Mangos (*Mangifera indica*) can be grown from St. Petersburg south or to the East Coast and must be planted in or near the water. They can also be grown in protected areas from Vera Beach to Fort Lauderdale. The mango, sometimes called the apple of the tropics, will take temperatures from 28 to 30 degrees but usually gets injured when not protected.

My mango tree in Tampa was frozen down to within a few feet of the ground. Is this something I should expect when cold temperatures prevail?

Unfortunately, mangos do get injured when unprotected. A few of them have produced fruit in protected courtyards in Tampa, but this is because of their proximity to the walls and the protection of the house from cold northern winds.

What kind of fertilizer should I use for my mango tree?

Use a citrus special. This can be a 4-6-8 or 4-8-8 or an equal number, such as 8-8-8, with a minor element package. Fertilize at the same time you would for citrus, usually spring, summer, and fall or, as a rough rule, February, June, and October.

Q What varieties of mango trees do you recommend for Florida?

A There are many good varieties to choose from. One of the older varieties, the Hayden, was considered the best for years. But today many other varieties have far surpassed the Hayden, such as the Tommy Atkins, Edward, Kent, and Parvin.

Q I have noticed a lot of little white bumps on the leaves of my mango tree, particularly where they attach to the stem. What is this?

A Your mango tree has scales. Scales are little insects that have a wax covering. They are difficult to control, and I recommend spraying with Malathion or another insecticide labeled for mangos.

Q I see banana trees growing all over Central and South Florida. Do they produce fruit here?

A They sure do. They aren't as long or as big as the ones you see in your local supermarket, which are shipped in from Central America. But if you have ever tasted a dwarf banana (*Musa* spp.), like the apple banana or the ladyfinger, you'll find out that what they lack in size they gain in flavor.

Q I heard that after a banana stalk comes on, I should cut off the bottom part where the bananas have formed. Is this true?

A Yes. After about two weeks the stalk has formed all of the bananas that it is going to. This is when you cut off the

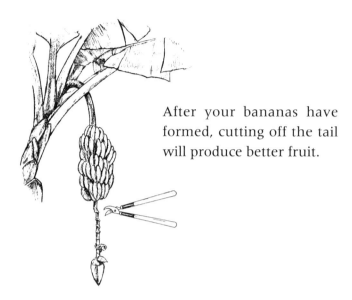

After your bananas have formed, cutting off the tail will produce better fruit.

bottom part, which is the male bloom or the tail. Doing this puts more energy into the fruit above.

Q Should I allow my bananas to ripen on the tree or cut them off before they ripen?

A Once the bananas are near maturity, cut them off and let them ripen just as they do commercially when shipping them from Central America.

Q How long does it take before banana trees are ready to set fruit?

A It usually takes about two years of frost-free weather for banana trees to start setting fruit. If there is a hard freeze, they may take an extra year to get back to where they were. This is one of the reasons there is more production in Central and South Florida than in North Florida.

Q Now that I see my banana trees starting to set some fruit, how long will it take from the time fruit starts to set until it is ripe?

A It normally takes quite a while, at least 120 days.

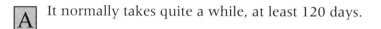

Q I came across an interesting fruit called the jaboticaba. What can you tell me about it?

A The jaboticaba (*Myrciaria cauliflora*) can grow to be fairly large, fifteen to twenty feet tall with a ten-foot spread. Normally grown in South Florida or in protected areas, it should be planted in full sun to partial shade. This small tree, or large bush, grows quite well in Florida.

Q My avocado tree is full of brown spots. What can I do about them?

A Your tree is suffering from a fungus problem called cercospora leaf spot. Spraying with neutral copper or another fungicide labeled for this problem will help.

Q I've heard that avocados take forever to produce fruit from seed. Is this true?

A It does take quite a while, anywhere from seven to ten years, for an ungrafted tree to produce fruit. That is one of the reasons avocados (*Persea americana*) are so often grafted.

Q What are some of the best cold-hardy varieties of avocados for Florida?

A There are a number of cold-hardy varieties, such as the Gainesville, the Young, and the Winter Mexican. These varieties will usually take temperatures down into the teens. There are some varieties that are not quite as cold tolerant, such as the Pollack, Simmonds, Booth 7, Booth 8, and Hall. These will take temperatures down into the upper twenties. Most avocados will be injured at about 32 degrees.

Q I just started an avocado by using three toothpicks to hold it in a glass of water. Which end should go up?

A The more pointed end should go up, with the rest of the seed floating in water.

An avocado can be started in a glass of water using toothpicks to hold it in place.

Q I would like to have a peach tree in my backyard. How well do they do in Florida?

A Peaches (*Prunus Persica*) can be grown here. They can reach a height of about twenty feet and have a spread of about fifteen feet. Unlike many of Florida's fruit trees, which are easily injured by the cold, peaches need a certain amount of cold weather. This limits them somewhat to North and Central Florida.

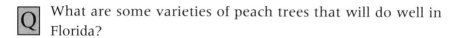

Q What are some varieties of peach trees that will do well in Florida?

A There are a few that do fairly well. The Florida One, the Jewel, and the Red Ceylon are old standards that have done well. Today's varieties that do well are grafted onto the Okinawa or the Nemaguard root stocks. You can also find other varieties, such as the Florida Sun and some of the Bell varieties.

Q I've heard peach trees don't last very long in Florida. Is this true?

A It all depends on what long is to you. Peach trees will last ten to fifteen years in Florida, and they never really go dormant.

Q I have noticed that my peach tree has a white scale on its leaves. Is this a common problem?

A Most peach trees are bothered by the San Jose scale at one time or another. Use an oil spray or Malathion during the dormant period to eradicate this problem.

Q Are there any guavas that grow well in Central Florida?

A There are quite a few. Personally, I like the Cattley guava (*Psidium littorale* var. *longipes*). It only reaches fifteen to twenty feet in height with a spread of ten to fifteen feet and is a little more bushy and shrublike than some of the older varieties. The purple-red fruit grows about one to one-and-a-half inches across.

Q Do the larger guavas grow here?

A Yes, they do. The large guava tree can reach twenty-five feet tall with a fifteen- to twenty-foot spread.

Q Are their any pear trees I can grow in Florida?

A You can grow some pears (*Pyrus* spp.) in the state of Florida. Normally varieties such as the Baldwin and the Orient, which have a crisp, white flesh, grow well in North Florida to some of the upper regions of Central Florida. There is also the Sand Pear, which is often used for cooking.

Q Can we grow raspberries here?

A Yes, there are some tropical raspberries that can be grown in Central and South Florida. Similar to tropical blackberries, they normally have thorny canes and a vining habit. Their reddish-purple fruit can be eaten fresh or made into delicious jams, jellies, and juice.

We have large bugs that look like they have shields on their backs attacking our raspberries. What should we do?

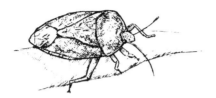

stink bug

 This is a stink bug or one of its cousins. To get rid of them, spray with Diazinon or Malathion.

 I have always enjoyed blackberry jam, can we grow blackberries in Florida?

 You certainly can grow blackberries in Florida. They are one of the most succulent fruits in our state.

 How much cold can tropical blackberries endure?

 Most of Florida's tropical blackberries can take temperatures down to about 26 degrees.

 Should I have more than one blackberry plant for better production?

 Yes. Blackberries are considered semifertile plants, meaning that one plant may produce, but it will do much better if it has a number of other blackberry plants nearby to help ensure pollination.

Q What kind of growing conditions do blueberries prefer?

A Blueberries require an acid soil with a pH of 4.2 to 5.2, which can be difficult to attain in Florida. Often this means adding plenty of organic matter, and if the pH is still too alkaline, adding sulfur or another form of soil acidifier.

Q What are some of the best varieties of blueberries for Florida?

A Try the Floridablue or the Sharpblue, which are grown from Gainesville north, although I have seen them growing a bit farther south when the soil has been amended.

Q I grew grapes in upstate New York. Can I grow the same ones here?

A You can grow grapes (*Vitis* spp.) well in Florida, but they won't be the same varieties you grew up North. Blue Lake, Lake Emerald, Norris, and Stover have all been adapted to Florida. I do not recommend the northern European bunch grapes because they frequently suffer from Pierce's disease and die within a year or two. However, the Muscadine varieties, such as Fry, Dixie, Cowart, Welder, and Southland, all do well.

I have heard that it is hard to get seedless grapes to grow in Florida. Is this true?

 Traditionally this has been the case. Most of the varieties that thrive here have a good bit of seeds along with fairly thick skin, at least this is the case for most of the Muscadines. However, there is now a variety available called the Orlando Seedless, which has large clusters of small, seedless fruit.

 I planted some seeds from a couple of kiwi fruit, but I'm not sure what to expect. What can you tell me about the kiwi?

 The seeds of the kiwi fruit germinate quite well when kept moist, although the process takes much longer than with other seeds. A native of New Zealand and Australia, the kiwi has been successfully grown in California and here in Florida. Growing the kiwi is similar to growing grapes on a trellis or wire system. They require a well-draining soil that has added organic matter. The kiwi does well in full sun and should be fertilized three or four times a year.

 I have a five-year-old guava tree in a pot on my back porch that has sooty mold on its leaves. Can you tell me what this problem is and how to treat it?

 This is black sooty mold, and it is caused by the wax scale. I recommend spraying the tree with a couple of applications of Malathion, about ten days to two weeks apart.

 I'm not sure how to control grass and weeds in our small citrus grove of twelve trees. The orange roots are so close to the surface of the ground that using a hoe or other sharp tool is out of the question, but I'm also concerned that a weed killer will be harmful to the trees. What do you suggest?

A You should be able to use a light scuffle hoe around the trees without too many problems. If the trunks are mature, it's safe to use a weed killer such as Round-Up as long as you keep it off the foliage and green stems. You could also use a weed trimmer to keep the grass and weeds trimmed back—just make sure to keep the cutting line away from the trunks.

Q What's the average age of a fruit tree bought at a nursery?

A Most of the time, trees that are available are two to three years old and at least three to five feet tall. Always verify the type of tree with the nurseryman because labels often drop off and can accidentally be reapplied to the incorrect tree. This problem is made easier by the fact that most nurseries put trees in blocks, the navels with navels, for example. You can also distinguish one variety from the other by breaking off a leaf to smell its aroma.

Q Should I add any organic matter to the soil before planting my fruit tree?

A You need to add peat moss, cow manure, and root stimulator to the root zone. Be sure to follow the label directions when using the root stimulator.

Q How big should I make the hole I am planting my fruit tree in?

A If you are adding soil amendments, I recommend digging the hole twice as wide as the container and at least as deep. This is because most trees' root zones are in the top area. In other words, the tree will spread wider than it will be deep.

Q I just bought a fruit tree, and when I removed it from the container, many of the roots were broken. What should I do?

A Anytime roots are broken or yellow or brown, take a pair of sterilized cutters and cut them off. If the roots appear diseased, a sterilizing solution should prevent the disease from spreading.

Q When planting my new fruit tree, should I add new soil or use a mixture of native soils?

A Take a shovel and make a homogenized mixture of native soil and added soil amendments, such as peat, cow manure, and other organic material. Put this around the root system of the newly planted tree. This will allow the best mix of water and minerals to be absorbed by the roots.

Q When I was transplanting my tree, I noticed that about 25 percent of the tree's top was injured. What should I do?

A It is not uncommon for a portion of the tree to get injured during transplanting. Remove the portion of the tree that was broken or damaged using clean cuts. This will help the tree repair itself and grow healthy and strong.

Q I just put in a peach tree, and the nurseryman recommended that I wrap some kind of tape around its trunk. What is the purpose of this tape?

A Fruit trees that are planted in the spring and summer are often wrapped with a trunk guard, which is the special tape you were shown. It is designed to keep the tree from getting sunburned or sun scald on its tender bark. Follow the nurseryman's advice; it will make the peach tree's adaptation process more successful.

Q I took a soil sample to my local county extension office, and they told me my soil's pH was too alkaline to plant my navel orange tree. The information pamphlet they gave me suggested I use sulfur, but the nurseryman sold me a soil acidifier. Is this the same thing?

A Yes, sulfur is a type of soil acidifier. Often the county extension service does not recommend name-brand products, which is why the pamphlet only mentioned sulfur in general. Depending on how alkaline your soil is, the soil acidifier you got should do the job when used according to label directions.

Q Can I grow apples here in Florida?

A There are a few varieties of apples (*Malus* spp.) that have adapted to Florida. The Anna and Golden Dorset will grow, but Floridians won't be putting northerners out of the apple business anytime soon. Our apples are much smaller, about the size of a small Red Delicious apple. Although you may not get quite the size of fruit you had hoped for, the apple tree will yield quite a production of crop.

Q Our apple trees have some spotting on their leaves. What causes this?

A This is a fungus problem, which is common for apples in Florida. This problem is experienced in other parts of the country but is more prevalent here because of our moisture and high humidity. We have to spray with a fungicide a bit more often, but rest assured, other parts of the country are applying their share of fungicides, too.

Q How should I trim my apple trees?

A Apple trees are normally trimmed according to a modified leader system. Every year you will trim out some of the branches, ones that cross over each other, allowing more sunlight to reach the center of the tree. This is normally done during the dormant season (January through early February).

Q My apple trees have a rustlike appearance on the foliage. What is this?

A This is called rust, and it is a type of fungus. It attacks a number of different plants, apples being one of them, throughout the state. Spraying with a fungicide such as Captan used according to label directions, will give you moderate results.

Q My apple tree turns a reddish-brown and then black. The nurseryman told me that this was a fire blight. What do I do?

A Fire blight is a bacterial disease that attacks the whole apple group. The normal procedure is to spray with an agricultural streptomycin, which is applied after pruning out any of the dead wood back into good wood. Between cuts, it is a good idea to disinfect your pruning shears in a 10 percent solution of bleach, or another disinfectant, and water.

Q Recently I came across a fruit called the star fruit. What can you tell me about it?

A The star fruit, also known as carambola, is grown mostly in Central and South Florida. It can reach heights of up to thirty feet with a fifteen- to twenty-five-foot spread. There are a number of varieties of carambola, including Golden Star, Peistao, Thayer, and Newcomb. These plants are admired for their golden, waxlike star-shaped fruit, which is often used in punches and other holiday drinks to float in the serving bowl. It has a sweet tangy flavor and is good for you.

Q I was told that the carambola fruit doesn't grow out on the limbs of the tree like most fruit. Where is it formed?

A The carambola fruit is formed on the branches and trunks of the tree, but not on the terminal growth like a citrus fruit.

I am going to plant a new carambola tree. Should I choose a sunny spot or a shady spot?

 Carmabola, like most fruit trees, produces best when planted in full sun. It would probably grow in your shady area, but production would be slow.

 I know carambolas are not cold hardy. Will it tolerate areas such as Clearwater or Dunedin in Central Florida?

 Young carambolas will tolerate temperatures down to 32 degrees Fahrenheit. The more mature carambola will adapt to short spells of temperatures that drop into the mid-twenties. If you plant this tree in Central Florida, cold protection should be part of your plan. Most people supply a heating source, such as blankets or a plastic cover (that cannot touch any part of the plant during a freeze) to protect their carambola.

 What is the best variety of blackberry for Florida?

 The variety of blackberry (*Rubus* spp.) that is most successful here is the Brazo. It does have thorns and, like most brambles, tends to take over the area in which it grows. The thorns are certainly a nuisance, but the fresh fruit and blackberry pies are your reward.

 How are blackberries usually planted?

You can buy gallon-sized, or larger, blackberry bushes from your local nursery. They may have to order them, or you may have to visit one of the nurseries that specializes in fruiting plants. You could also visit the annual sale at one of the botanical gardens or the Rare Fruit Council show to purchase your blackberry plant.

 When is the best time to trim back my blackberries?

 The best time to trim them back is during the dormant season (January). You'll want to trim them back quite a bit (about one half), and be sure to wear long sleeves and a good pair of leather gloves.

 Can I grow blueberries in Florida?

 Blueberries (*Vaccinium* spp.) can be grown here, but they prefer an acid soil. Because there are few naturally occurring acid areas in Florida, you'll almost certainly need to use an acid-forming fertilizer. Check the pH of your soil and adjust it where you can. Also, select varieties such as Sharpblue or Floridablue, which are the most well adapted to our state.

 When growing blueberries, should I start with just a few plants or would planting a lot of them give me better results?

 I suggest trying just a few to see how successful they will grow for you. Once you are successful, you can make your crop bigger next season.

I would like to grow my own Barbados cherry. Is this possible in Florida?

 You'll have the best luck if you live in South Florida. You can grow them in Central Florida, but they must be protected. It will get injured when temperatures reach freezing. The Barbados cherry (*Eugenia uniflora*) can grow ten to twelve feet high with an eight- to ten-foot spread. These cherries are known to have high concentrations of vitamin C, making it a delicious fruit and a favorite of the health conscious.

 Is a well-draining soil important for citrus trees?

 Drainage is vital for citrus. When planting them, mound the soil as much as six inches where you will place the tree. Be sure to plant the citrus at the same depth as it was growing in the container.

 How important is it for my citrus to have a bump at the graft union?

 You don't necessarily need to see a bump, but there should be a distinguishable area where the graft union took place. It can sometimes be a side graft, where you can actually see where the root stock was placed on the side and grafted onto it from the scion. There is also a noticeable difference in wood color at the graft sight. Citrus can be bud grafted or cleft grafted using a small piece of bud.

Q I have looked at a number of citrus trees and a few of them look rough at the base. Is this something to be concerned about?

A When buying a citrus or any other grafted plant, make sure there is a good graft union. It should be clean, smooth, and well healed. Also, make sure there is no dead wood in the tree.

Q I was told not to use a high nitrogen fertilizer on my citrus trees in the fall. Why is this?

A The only reason you don't want to do this in the fall is because it would stimulate new growth, which can be easily injured by the impending cold weather.

Q What do we do for our citrus and other plants when cold wintery days are followed by a warming trend?

A This is definitely a problem in Florida, and it often happens in December and January. Many plants start to pop out with new growth only to be severely injured by a cold spell. Follow the weather reports closely during these times. You can protect your plants using blankets, sheets, and even small light bulbs under these covers to help raise the temperature a few degrees.

Q My citrus tree has a crooked trunk. Is this cause for alarm?

A It is not uncommon for citrus trees to have a bulge at their base. In general, when buying citrus, you should try to get one with a nice, straight, clean trunk. But your tree's crooked trunk should not pose any specific problems.

Q Are there any tips you can give me for harvesting my citrus fruit?

A Leave the fruit on the tree until it is mature in size, has a good color, and has a smooth texture. There is a definite season for harvesting citrus, so make sure to allow the fruit to hang on the tree for as long as possible. Some early varieties, such as navels and Hamlins, will be harvested early in the season (October and November). The mid-season varieties, such as the Valencia, will be harvested late in the season.

Q My citrus tree is full of a black sooty mold. What does this mean?

A This is the most commonly asked question related to citrus. The black sooty mold you see indicates an insect problem, such as aphids, white flies, or scales, sometimes even a combination of all of these. Spraying should be done before the problem gets out of hand. Use Malathion or another insecticide labeled for citrus.

Q We have a small backyard but would love to grow grapefruit. Will this tree be too big for us?

A Grapefruit trees (*Citrus* x *paradisi*) do grow to be fairly large. It is not uncommon for them to reach heights of thirty or forty feet and spread up to thirty feet. You would need to keep this tree trimmed down, but you could do this and still have a nicely balanced shape.

Q We would like to plant a white grapefruit that doesn't have many seeds. Which variety do you recommend?

A The Marsh is considered a seedless variety, though it may have a few seeds. Seedless usually means only one to five seeds are present, but this is nothing compared to the Duncan, which can have as many as sixty seeds.

Q We were considering planting a pink or red grapefruit. What are our options?

A For a pink grapefruit, the Thompson pink is a good choice. For a red grapefruit, the Ruby red is successfully grown here. The flavor, in my opinion, does not vary much between the two. Many people just like the different colored pulp, whether it be pink, red, or white.

Q Can we grow Key limes successfully in the St. Petersburg area?

A Certainly. Remember that, like most citrus, lime trees (*Citrus aurantiifolia*) usually have thorns. Key limes are not cold hardy and need to be protected in North and Central Florida. As a matter of fact, in North Florida, these trees should be container plants. The lime tree will get injured at 32 degrees Fahrenheit and can be critically injured when temperatures fall in the low twenties for any length of time.

What is the most common lemon grown here?

 That would be the Meyer. It is the one most similar to the lemons (*Citrus Limon*) purchased at the supermarket. Many people also grow the large Ponderosa lemon, or Florida Pilamen, because it grows to six or seven inches in size, almost as big as a grapefruit.

 We would like to grow citrus in the Pensacola area. Is this possible?

 Yes, it is possible. You can grow tangerines, which have a great flavor. This tree will grow to twenty feet with a fifteen-foot spread. The Dancy and Clementine are the most cold-hardy varieties. You can also grow kumquats. The kumquat (*Fortunella* spp.) is cold hardy and great for marmalades. They grow up to fifteen feet with a ten-foot spread. The Meiwa is a hybrid variety; it is rounded and has a sweet flavor and an edible flesh and skin. These are only about one inch long. Because they are cold hardy, Kumquats make great marmalade.

 I'm looking for an early-season juice orange. Do you have any suggestions?

 The Hamlin is one of the best early juice oranges. It will often ripen in October and continue to produce until December. The fruit is smooth skinned, it has very few seeds, and it is one of the most popular early juice oranges.

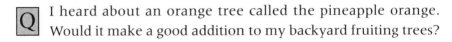 **Q** I heard about an orange tree called the pineapple orange. Would it make a good addition to my backyard fruiting trees?

A The pineapple orange is rather seedy, but it is a delicious fruit, either eaten by hand or for juicing. Normally it ripens from December through March.

Q I have heard about a variety of orange called the Parson-Brown. Is it good for juicing?

A The Parson-Brown is another tasty orange that is often used for its juice. It has a rather rough skin and normally ripens from October through December.

Q Are tangelos a hybrid cross?

A Tangelos (*Citrus* x *Tangelo*) are a cross between a grapefruit and a tangerine. Tangerines (*Citrus reticulata*) are easy to eat from sections, and grapefruits, of course, give us the largest fruit possible.

Q I recently purchased a tangelo that has a neck at the top of the fruit. What variety is this?

A This is the Minneola tangelo. It can be harvested anywhere from January through March and has a pear-shaped body with reddish-orange flesh.

Q I saw a tiny fruit that looks like a very small orange or tangerine. What kind of fruit is this?

A This is the calamondin. This tree grows between ten and eighteen feet tall with a ten- to fifteen-foot spread. They have small, orange fruit and are mostly grown as ornamentals.

Q We have a citrus tree that has a wartlike scab on its foliage. What is this and what can we do for it?

A This is a fungus disease called scab. It can become a serious problem if left to spread. Spraying with neutral or liquid copper should help keep this under control. Apply a prebloom spray if scab has been a problem in the past.

Q Our oranges have a brownish cast on their skins. What causes this?

A This is the tiny citrus rust mite. Although it does cause the orange's skin to have a brown color, the fruits are not harmful to eat. You may notice that the fruit is smaller in size because of the mites' feeding activity. Spraying with a miticide should help control them.

Q We have an orange tree that has a lot of spotting on the foliage that looks like grease. What is this?

A This is the greasy spot fungus. Spraying with neutral copper or another fungicide labeled for citrus should help with this problem. Next season, spray as a preventative measure.

Q My navel orange tree's leaves have a fluffy material, almost like a white fly, on them. Can you identify this for me?

A You have either cottony cushion scale or a woolly white fly. Typically, white fly has tiny silvery dots behind the leaves. You will notice a woolly appearance near and around these dots. Spraying with Malathion or an oil spray, such as Ethion or Volck oil, should help with woolly white fly or scale.

Q There is a white material that looks like white paraffin on my citrus. What is this?

A This is wax scale, which gets its name from its waxy appearance. Scales can be difficult to control, but spraying with an oil spray or Malathion, according to label directions, should help.

Q What can you tell us about growing pineapple?

A Pineapples (*Ananas comosos*) are bromeliads and are easily grown in Florida. Their biggest drawback is that they are not cold hardy. The pineapple is best planted in large containers, at least five gallons, so they can be brought in from the cold. The pineapple needs approximately one-and-a-half years from the time it is started until the time it will start to produce another pineapple. To force bloom, you will need ten to twelve grains of calcium carbide to put into the bud. Normally done in the warmer months, this is called gassing. It should speed up the fruit production by as much as five to seven months. Calcium carbide can normally be found at many hobby shops or hunting and camping supply stores.

Q If I use the fruit bought from the store to start my pineapple, how much of the top of the plant should be removed with the green crown section?

A You'll want to take off a good inch of meat with the crown portion of the pineapple. Allow it to dry for one full day and then plant it into soil.

Q I heard that a pineapple dies after it produces fruit. Is this true?

A This is true, but in some cases the pineapple lasts for a long period of time before its demise. After it has produced a fruit, it will send up many side shoots. From these, you can get an even larger production of fruit. Most people don't even realize their pineapple died because they assume these side shoots are the same plant. Actually, they are the next generation of pineapples.

Q How far apart should our pineapples be planted?

A Pineapples need about four feet between plants so be sure to give them plenty of space.

Q How big does a pineapple grow?

A The pineapples grown in Florida backyards normally grow anywhere from eighteen inches to three feet tall. They can get slightly larger, though.

Q The papayas that I have grown in the past grow well but are injured each year by the cold. Is there something I can do to prevent injury?

A Papayas (*Carica* spp.) are a true tropical fruit and are best left for growing in South Florida. Many of us living in the central part of the state can grow them in containers, which allows them to be protected. Planting next to a wall or close to the side of your home will certainly make a difference in the amount of heat protection. Living on or near the water will also help protect the papaya. Temperatures of 32 degrees or below, which most of the state experiences except for the Keys, will injure this plant. However, if cut back after injury, they usually resprout and give good fruit.

Q My friend is growing a huge papaya tree that's almost twenty feet tall. Do they normally get this big?

A Most of them do grow fifteen to twenty feet tall. If you are looking for a smaller variety, I recommend some of the dwarf varieties, such as the Hawaiian Solo.

Q When I dug up my papaya, I noticed the roots were full of knots. Is this normal?

A This is the work of nematodes. Add a lot of organic matter, which will break down into a good humus, to feed the more beneficial bacterias that will feed on the nematodes.

Q My papaya fruit look great on the tree, but when I cut them open they are full of maggots. Can you help me with this repulsive problem?

A These maggots are from a fruit fly that bothers the papaya. Often the only solution is to place plastic bags over the fruit when they are small and allow them to develop inside the bag. This is fairly labor intensive, but it's well worth it for that delicious tasting papaya.

Q My friend wants to give me a Japanese plum. How big can I expect it to grow?

A Japanese plum (*Eriobotrya japonica*), or loquats, are medium-sized trees, reaching heights of twenty to thirty feet with a spread of fifteen to twenty feet. Personally, I find them quite messy, but they do have an excellent tasting fruit. Many people grow them for their ornamental value.

Q I would like to buy a loquat tree. Are there any varieties that you recommend?

A Some varieties that flourish in Florida are the Fletcher, Oliver, Premier, Wolfe, and Golden Nugget.

Q What are the best varieties of figs grown in Florida?

A The Brown Turkey and Celeste are two of the best varieties of figs (*Ficus* spp.) for Florida. Many people have grown varieties from other parts of the country, and these have met with varying degrees of success.

Q Do I need to add organic matter around my fig trees?

 A Yes. Figs have problems with nematodes and microscopic eel-worms, and they need heavy, organic mulch to produce bacteria that feed upon these creatures. Also, make sure you pick a bright, sunny spot where your fig will receive six hours of sunlight daily.

Q My fig trees have a rustlike material on them. What is this?

 A This is a rust fungus. Figs and rust fungus seem to go hand in hand in Florida. It is a good idea to spray with liquid copper when the fruits are half mature with new leaves. This will cut down on the rust fungus disease.

Q Recently I tasted an unusual fruit called litchi. Does it grow well in Florida?

A The litchi (*Litchi chinensis*), a native of China, is a round-headed tree that has leathery, shiny green leaves. Its fruit, sometimes called the litchi nut, has a hard, leathery skin that turns bright red when ripe. The flesh inside is white and has an excellent flavor. It can be eaten fresh or frozen. The litchi tree normally grows twenty to thirty feet tall with a comparable spread. The most popular variety in Florida is the Brewster.

Q How tender is the litchi tree in cold weather?

A Tender young trees can be damaged at 28 degrees Fahrenheit and should be protected in most of Central Florida. Older, more mature trees will survive temperatures in the twenties.

Q When does a litchi fruit ripen?

A The litchi fruit ripens in June and July. Mulching is quite important for this tree. It helps conserve moisture, which in turn yields a better crop.

Q My litchi tree's leaves are all spotted. What causes this?

A Litchis are susceptible to spider mites. You can control them with Malathion or another insecticide labeled for this use.

9

PALMS

One of the first visual images people have when they think of Florida is palm trees. Along with beaches, citrus trees, and sunset vistas, palm trees are a symbol of the Sunshine State.

Palms add a slender gracefulness that is hard to find in almost any hard wood. One reason is that they are so radically different in their growing habits from a dicot plant. Palm trees are monocot, meaning they have a single seed leaf as opposed to a bean or an oak, which have two seed leaves. Also, palms do not have cambium layers. Instead, they have vascular bundles. In other words, if you cut a palm tree in half, you would see a thousand little straws. By their very nature, palms are unique trees whose tropical and stately appearance is an integral part of the ambiance of the Florida landscape.

 I've heard that palm trees are very tolerant of dry conditions. Is this true?

 It depends on the type of palm tree and its size. Most palms are drought tolerant, but there also palms that actually grow in water. What is important is that palms do well in most of our Florida sands and soils and are well suited to our climate.

Q We have some newly planted palms. How often should we water them?

A Like any other newly planted plant, you should water them every few days at first. Once they become established, you can water them as little as once a week, and eventually, if the soil is moist, you may be able to water them on an as-needed basis.

Q We have a Queen palm that seems to be crinkling on the top. What is causing this and what can I do about it?

A Your Queen palm (*Arecastrum Romanzoffianum* var. *australe*) has a manganese deficiency. A couple of pounds of manganese sulfate should be able to solve your problem. Remember, palms are slow in their assimilation, so it will take a few months, maybe as long as six, for this deficiency to rectify itself.

Q We have a Canary Island date palm, and the entire older bottom row of fronds is turning yellow. Should we fertilize it?

A Yellowing on the bottom row usually indicates a magnesium deficiency. You need to give your palm a palm food or a general 6-6-6 fertilizer. Apply equal amounts of manganese, magnesium, and a general fertilizer. For a larger palm, apply four or five pounds of each.

Q I have noticed that many of the fronds on my palms seem to grow naturally old, turn yellow, and die. I'd like to remove them. Is there an appropriate time to cut them off?

A The best time to cut off the fronds is when they turn yellow to light green in color. Once they become totally brown, it takes longer with a lot more work to cut them off with a typical palm saw.

Q Every year our local art group uses the palm trees to hammer ropes to for hanging signs and banners, and every year we seem to be losing more palms. Could this be the problem?

A It certainly could. By putting nails into the trunks of the trees, you are increasing their chances of ganoderma, which is a deadly fungus. I recommend tying the ropes around the trunks of the palms to hang the signs if you want them to survive.

Q Our palm has a big mushroom growing out of its base. What is it?

A It is the fruiting body of the fungus ganoderma. Ganoderma has a fruiting body of half a mushroom to a full mushroom and is lethal to a tree.

A ganoderma mushroom growing out of the base of a palm tree can be deadly.

Q We recently cut down one of our large palms, and we noticed large holes throughout the bud of the tree. What caused these big holes?

A The holes were caused by the palm weevil, the largest of the weevils in Florida. As they make their holes through the palm's bud, they kill it. If you catch it early and spray with an insecticide such as Lindane, you should be able to save the palm.

Q I noticed a sawdust material on the fronds of my palms. What is causing this?

A The problem is called palm leaf skeletonizer. It is caused by the larva of a moth that eats the leaflets of the frond, turning them into this sawdustlike material. Spraying with Sevin, Diazinon, or Dursban, according to label directions, should help control the larva.

Q I'm seeing some browning on the tips of the leaves of my palm tree. What causes this?

A Browning on the tips of your palm leaves, like with most plants, is normally due to the soil drying out excessively. Palms are fairly drought tolerant, but smaller palms and those that are growing in containers need more water than palms that are fifty to sixty feet tall and living in their natural habitat.

Q We are considering moving a palm tree in our yard from one section to another. We were told that it is important to keep the bud and fronds tied together. Is this true?

A The biggest problem in moving a palm, whether it is fifty feet or fifty miles, is keeping the bud from being injured. That's why tying up the fronds is so important.

Q We have a palm that has thorns poking out of its trunk. If it weren't for this, we would think that it was a Queen palm. What kind of palm do we have?

A Palms that look similar to Queen palms but have needlelike structures along the base of the trunk are Gru-gru palms (*Acrocomia* spp.). Mostly seen in Central and South Florida, the Gru-gru palm can grow to be forty or fifty feet tall. The menacing appearance of these spikes are always a conversation piece.

Gru-gru palms have unusual spikes at the base of their trunks.

Q Our Queen palm has a lot of cracks in its bark. Should we be concerned?

A Cracks are not a major problem. They may go back to an old freeze injury. I recommend spraying the trunks with a fungicide from time to time—say, every six months to a year. This will keep out any secondary disease that could occur in the cracks.

Q We were recently in the Sarasota area and saw a baby royal palm. Could you tell us more about this tree?

A The baby royal palm (*Roystonia* spp.) is often confused with the Manila palm (*Veitchia Merrillii*), which is sometimes called the Christmas palm because of its bright red cluster of fruit. The baby royal will reach twenty to twenty-five feet, which makes it about half the size of the large royal palm.

Q There is a palm called chamaedorea that we used to grow up North as an indoor plant. Can it be grown as an outside plant here in Florida?

A The chamaedorea can be grown outside in protected areas, but is normally not seen outside any farther north than Pinellas County. It is one of the few palms that folks have known as an indoor plant but can grow outside as well.

Q We have a cane palm and noticed that some of the tree looks a little yellow. What should we do for it?

A The cane palm (*Chrysalidocarpus lutescens*), sometimes called the areca palm, is often used as a potted plant in cooler areas where it must be protected, although I have seen it used as a landscape plant in Central and South Florida. You need to increase the amount of manganese and magnesium it is getting. You should give this along with a palm food and a general 6-6-6 or an 8-8-8 fertilizer.

Q Here in Miami, we recently lost the majority of our coconut palms to a disease called lethal yellowing. We replaced them with a dwarf Malayan variety that is doing amazingly well. Why is this?

A   Years ago many of the coconut palms (*Cocos nucifera*) were devastated in South Florida by this lethal yellowing disease. Luckily, some varieties seem to be immune to this problem, and the Malayan dwarf palm is one of them. Although it doesn't grow to a height of seventy-five feet or more like some of the coconut palms, it is an adequate size for the average one-story Florida home.

Q   While looking for a palm to grow outside in North Florida, we heard of the Chinese fan palm. Could you tell us something about it?

A   The Chinese fan palm (*Livistona chinensis*) is a medium-sized palm, about twenty-five to thirty-five feet in height, that can be grown in North, Central, and South Florida. It is a rather cold-hardy tree with unique fanlike fronds that curl over to give it a graceful appearance.

Q   We have a palm in our backyard that we were told was a paurotis palm. Could you tell us more about it?

A   The paurotis palm (*Acoelorrhaphe Wrightii*), sometimes called the saw cabbage palmetto, is a native of the Everglades. This clumping palm grows well in wet areas but will grow in higher, dry soils as well. It has a high salt tolerance and grows in full sun to partial shade.

Q   We are looking for a palm that will stay between eight and fourteen feet high. What do you recommend?

A   For Central and South Florida I recommend the pygmy date palm (*Phoenix Roebelenii*). This graceful palm looks very much like its *Phoenix* cousins. Like its larger relatives, the pygmy date palm has a thorn that grows two-and-a-half to three inches in size at its base. It makes a great entryway plant or a small specimen plant in the landscape. In North and Central Florida, where the temperatures can drop down into the teens, it should be protected with cover.

Q I recently came across a palm with striking blue-green fronds. I was told it was a jelly palm, so named because it could be used for making jelly. Is this true?

A The jelly palm (*Butia capitata*), sometimes called the pindo palm, is one of the most cold-hardy palms grown in Florida. You can see them growing throughout North and South Florida. Their graceful, blue-green fronds make them a good specimen tree. And yes, you can actually make jelly from their fruit.

Q We are looking for a small fan palm that will be cold hardy, preferably something ten to fifteen feet tall. What do you recommend?

A I recommend the European fan palm (*Chamaerops humilis*), a native of southern Europe that can be grown in North, Central, and South Florida. It is tolerant of many different soils and sands and grows best in partial shade to full sun. The European fan palm is occasionally grown in a bright lobby as an indoor plant. It is the only fan palm that grows fifteen feet or less.

Q I have seen a palm with a stout trunk that is almost three feet across. I think it is attractive and would like to get one. What is it called?

A No doubt, it is one of the Canary Island date palms (*Phoenix canariensis*). It is one of the most beautiful specimen palms in the state, which is why it is often used as an avenue tree or landscape specimen. Because it reaches fifty to sixty feet high spreads about thirty feet, it needs plenty of room to grow. It gets its nickname, the pineapple palm, from the diamondlike patterns sometimes formed on its trunk. If you plant this tree, be wary of the four- to six-inch long thorns on the bases of the large fronds.

Q I'm looking for a cold-hardy clump palm that I can grow in North Florida. What should I choose?

A I recommend the lady palm (*Rhapis Excelsa*), which will grow in full sun to partial shade. It is not very salt tolerant but is a good cold-hardy clump palm, making it a good palm for North to Central Florida.

Q Is it true that Florida's state tree is the cabbage palmetto?

A Yes, and for good reason. The cabbage palmetto (*Livistona australis*) grows from one tip of the state to the other. This native has been here at least as long as man has inhabited Florida. It is salt tolerant and will often grow right down into the water. The cabbage palmetto grows wild in almost every type of situation and reaches heights of sixty to eighty feet. I can't think of another palm that can be seen growing in such great abundance from Tallahassee to the Florida keys.

Q I haven't seen Washingtonian palms grown much here. Why is this?

A The Washingtonian is used here in Florida. It is unequaled for avenue plantings, but it can outgrow the landscape, sometimes growing more than seventy-five feet. This enormous size makes it too large for small properties and makes it difficult to keep the old fronds trimmed, which is why most large specimens have a petticoat to them.

Q Our Washingtonians aren't growing very quickly. Is this normal?

A Most palms are slow in their assimilation and relatively slow in their growth habits when compared to some of the dicot trees like maples or oaks. Although the Washingtonian palms do not grow with such vigorous spurts, they do grow well once established. So don't worry.

Q We were told that mulching around palms is not a good idea. Is this true?

A Mulching can be done successfully around palms, but as with many plants, holding moisture up against the trunk for a long period of time can increase fungus problems. For that reason, I do not recommend mulching around palms. If you do decide to mulch your palms, try to keep it as far away from the trunk as possible.

Q I have heard that bud rot is a serious problem for palms. Is there anything we can do to prevent it?

A Bud rot on palms is normally a secondary problem that occurs after the bud has been injured. Your best preventative measure is to try to keep the palm bud free from injury when you are moving and trimming it. Also, if you see problems with the bud, such as spotting at the top of the crown of the palm, spray with a fungicide.

10

VINES AND
GROUND COVERS

Almost everyone has an area around their house they want to hide or a piece of unmanageable landscape they would rather just cover over. You might be tired of looking at your neighbor's 1950 Chevy (sitting on cinder blocks, of course) or maybe you have a utility area full of garbage cans that is practical in purpose but offensive to the eye. You may have an area of your yard that slopes so steeply mowing defies the laws of physics, or you may just be plain old tired of mowing the lawn week after week. And what is the solution to all of these annoyances? Plants, of course!

A vining plant is the cheapest and most attractive way to hide an unsightly vista. But more than just blocking out unwanted views, vines also block out the fierce summer sun and lessen the excessive heat on patios, providing shade with a minimum of care, effort, and money. There are vines for your every need and want. You can find vines that thrive in full sun and in partial shade, all the while growing well in our sandy soil. You may want a sweet-scented vine, such as the Confederate jasmine (*Jasminum* spp.), or you may want a vine that adds a splash of color to your landscape, such as the bougainvillea. When it comes to vines in Florida, the possibilities are practically endless.

Speaking of economical and attractive, you can't beat a good ground cover for those frustrating problem areas of the landscape. And ground covers have the added bonus of being great energy savers; they absorb the sunlight, shade the ground, and prevent reflected light from heating the home. When the shade of your large oak tree makes it nearly impossible to grow grass, a bed of Boston ferns (*Nephrolepis exaltata* var. 'Bostoniensis') cures your problem and adds a picturesque element to your yard. And when you have run out of patience with that steep slope to the sidewalk, planting the delicately fragrant but tenacious honeysuckle (*Lonicera* spp.) will allow you to relax and forget about it. From flowering ground covers to spreading plants that can cover some of the sandiest, hottest areas in the Florida yard, these plants will cut your work in half and beautify your yard at the same time.

Q We have a beautiful yellow vine with bell-shaped, waxy flowers that are about four inches across. What is this and how big will it get?

A You have an allamanda, one of Florida's most showy vines. This vine can reach heights of eight to ten feet with a spread of about the same. An allamanda will grow well in full sun to light shade, and they are sensitive to temperatures of less than 20 degrees, so they should be planted in protected areas. I do have one cautionary note: Allamandas have a cathartic effect and can act as a purge so they need to be planted out of the reach of small children.

Q We have a beautiful Coral vine, but it is growing too prolifically. How can we keep it in check?

A The Coral vine (*Antigonon leptopus*) is a very fast-growing vine. When it is through blooming, which it does almost all year long, cut it back to keep it from growing out of control.

Q We love the orchid tree, and we were told that there is a vine related to it. I would like to plant this at our home in Miami. Will it do well here?

A Yes. The Bauhinia vine is ideal for protected areas of Central and South Florida. Its exquisite, dark red flowers do closely resemble those of the Bauhinia tree. Because it is a vine, it must be trained to grow on some type of support, such as a trellis. This plant is sometimes injured by frost, but it usually comes back.

Q We recently saw a beautiful bougainvillea vine at the Sunken Gardens in St. Petersburg. Would it grow as impressively in our own backyard?

A There are a number of species of the bougainvillea, and they are all welcome additions to the Florida home. It is available in brilliant shades of deep pink, almost-red, orange, white, and yellow. Bougainvillea can reach up to fifty feet in the landscape, but it also does well in hanging baskets and as a patio plant. It can even be trimmed into a fairly thick shrub. Although in most of Central and North Florida it will be injured by frost, it usually bounces back well. The bougainvillea needs regular feedings with a fertilizer low in nitrogen and high in phosphorus and potassium. Because this plant has thorns, I recommend planting it in an area where there is not much traffic.

Q My bougainvillea is in a hanging basket and is growing way too far out. Can I trim it back?

A Often in a controlled environment, the bougainvillea, as well as most other vines, will have to be trimmed to be kept in bounds. However, because the bougainvillea is a flowering plant and you don't want to interfere with blooming, do not trim any more than you have to.

Bougainvillea growing in a hanging basket.

Q Someone told me that my bougainvillea will die in temperatures lower than 40 degrees. Is this true?

A No. Bougainvilleas can take temperatures down to freezing and will, in fact, take temperatures down into the twenties and even the teens. There will be some damage below 32 degrees, but at 40 degrees, there isn't even any leaf drop.

Q My bougainvillea is looking a bit yellow, although the veins are remaining green. What is causing this?

A There are a number of possibilities. Check the pH of the soil because it may be too alkaline. Adding a little soil acidifier will help if this is the problem. A native of Mexico, the bougainvillea will tolerate a fairly high pH, but sometimes Florida's is just too much.

Q Which vines can take the Florida heat on the west side of my home?

 A You might consider the bougainvillea, the climbing fig (*Ficus pumila*), roses, morning-glory (*Calystegia* spp.), or even the Boston ivy (*Parthenocissus tricuspidata*). The latter two will take the shade as well as the Florida sun. One of the most popular vines that takes full sun is the Carolina jasmine (*Gelsemium* spp.).

Q I know flowering roses are a vining plant for some states, but do they fare well in Florida?

A There are a number of attractive vining roses that do well in Florida, for example, the Don Juan. I grew a Don Juan for fifteen years without spraying much at all.

Q I have a bleeding-heart that was given to me by my late aunt, and I would like to keep it growing. Is it easy to propagate?

A The bleeding-heart (*Clerodendrum Thomsoniae*) can be started by cuttings and by layering. It can survive in most areas of the state, growing in North, Central, and South Florida. The bleeding-heart does well on a trellis or fence.

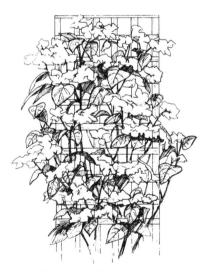

Bleeding-hearts grow well on a trellis.

187

Q What is the fastest growing annual vine in Florida?

A Moonflower (*Ipomoea alba*) and the morning-glory (*Calystegia* spp.), raised from seeds, grow quickly. Although with the morning-glory, the perennial is preferred because it will flower year after year.

Q What can you tell us about the garlic vine?

A The garlic vine is a South American plant that does well in Florida. It has a beautiful pink flower that is sometimes veined with a rose or purple coloration. Often grown from seed, the garlic vine should be protected from the cold. It is normally planted in the spring and will flower from summer through fall, reaching a height of eight feet with a comparable spread.

Q We have a wall that we have tried to grow vines on with little success. Can you recommend a vine that will grow well on a concrete wall without forcing the mortar out from between the bricks?

A You might consider the climbing fig (*Ficus pumila*), or creeping fig, which can spread fifteen to twenty feet and grow up to fifteen feet high. The fact that it is aggressive and attractive makes it a popular choice for commercial buildings, such as offices and restaurants.

Q Do you recommend the fatshedera for my home in Central Florida?

 A The fatshedera is a cross between the Japanese aralia (*Aralia* spp.) and English ivy (*Hedera Helix*) and is sometimes called aralia ivy. This evergreen botanical wonder is a vining shrub that grows as high as ten feet and features rich, dark-green foliage. It will need some support to climb. The fatshedera is injured by temperatures below freezing, but it can be grown in Central Florida. Try growing this impressive plant against a wall or in a protected corner or in an indoor porch or patio.

 Q Can most vines be planted against a wooden wall?

A I do not recommend planting any vine against a wooden wall because it will hold moisture, increasing the chance of a mold or fungus problem. If you are going to make some type of trellis, construct a hinged structure that can be pulled away from the wooden wall.

 Q My Boston ivy's leaves are turning brown in some areas, and I have noticed a bit of webbing. What might be the cause?

A Most of the time, these signs on the Boston ivy (*Parthenocissus tricuspidata*) point to a mite problem. A spider mite is very tiny, only about one-fiftieth of an inch, and causes webbing. Spraying with a miticide should help. If your ivy is indoors, you can use a fifty-fifty alcohol-water solution applied with a cotton swab.

189

Q I am looking for a vine that doesn't have too many disease or insect problems. What do you recommend?

 A Although almost every plant has a few problems, the closest thing you are going to find to problem-free is the Carolina jasmine (*Gelsimium* spp.). It can be grown anywhere in Florida in full sun to partial shade, reaching a height of about ten feet and spreading about the same. You rarely find a Carolina jasmine with an insect or fungus problem. This fact, along with its bright green foliage and beautiful yellow flowers, makes Carolina jasmine highly recommended for the Florida yard.

 Q My Carolina jasmine is getting a bit leggy. What can I do for this?

 A If the Carolina jasmine (*Gelsimium* spp.) is planted in full sun, this is not usually a problem. If it is planted in partial shade and becomes leggy, trim back major branches so the plant can branch out more. This will make for a bushier plant.

 Q I have been trying to root some English ivy, but it always seems to die. What am I doing wrong?

 A English ivy (*Hedera Helix*) can be started like many plants. Your chances will be greatly increased if you get some rooting hormone from your local nurseryman. Start your plant in a plastic or clay pot filled with good potting soil. Then, either put a plastic bag over the pot or put it in the shade. This creates a mini-greenhouse, which keeps the moisture level higher. This will almost certainly get your ivy to root.

Q I have some English ivy growing underneath an oak tree. I recently noticed a lot of brown spots on the leaves. What is this?

A This is a fungus problem. Spray the area with a fungicide, and try watering so that the water is not falling on the foliage on a constant basis.

Q Is it possible to grow clematis in Florida?

A Clematis, and there are a number of species of this plant, can be grown in Florida, but it is normally not recommended. Perhaps a variety of clematis will one day be developed that is better adapted to Florida, but until then, you are wise to choose a vining plant more suited to our growing conditions.

Q I have grown philodendrons as house plants for years, but I think I recently saw one growing on top of a pine tree. Is this possible?

A It sure is. Philodendrons love plenty of water and sunlight, and what better place to find these than at the top of a tree? The small potted plant you grow at home can develop into monstrous proportions in the right growing conditions.

Q My morning-glory has a flower that changes from blue to purple to pink. Is this degree of color change normal?

A There are different types of morning-glories (*Calystegia* spp.). In general, the morning-glory changes from early morning to

191

mid-day to late in the afternoon, and often the flower color will change as well. Luckily for us, these flowers bloom six to eight months out of the year and are vigorous growers. It also makes a great plant for the gardener who wishes to have a large area covered in a short period of time.

Q We saw a wood rose growing in Hawaii. Can we grow it here in Florida as well?

A The wood rose (*Rosa gymnocarpa*) can be grown in Central and South Florida. It is not cold hardy and will be injured by freezing temperatures, but it will normally grow back from the base. The wood rose gets its name from the appearance of its seed pods, which resemble carved wooden roses.

Q The Virginia creeper and poison ivy look similar to me. How can I tell the difference?

A The easiest way to tell these two plants apart is by the number of leaves. The Virginia creeper (*Parthenocissus quinquefolia*) has five leaflets, and the poison ivy (*Rhus radicans*) only has three.

Q I have heard the word *gourd* used in a number of ways. What does it actually refer to?

A The name gourd often refers to cucurbits, which are plants akin to the pumpkin (*Cucurbita* spp.), cucumber (*Cucumis sativus*), and melon (*Cucumis* spp.). Some of the more common gourds are the white-flowering gourd (*Lagenaria siceraria*); the snake, or serpent, gourd (*Trichosanthes Anguina*); the white, or wax, gourd (*Benincasa hispida*); and the dishcloth gourd (*Luffa aegyptiaca*). Many of these gourds have unusual shapes, and they are normally grown along fences, on trellises, or staked.

Q Will the trumpet honeysuckle grow as well in Florida as it does in Georgia?

A It is a Florida native and should grow about as well in most of North and Central Florida as it does in Georgia. The trumpet honeysuckle (*Lonicera sempervirens*) is known for its dense foliage, beautiful red, tubular flowers tinged with yellow, and its unmistakable scent.

Q Can the passion fruit be grown in Florida?

A The passion fruit comes from the passion vine (*Passiflora edulis*), which is quite an attractive, rapid grower. The fruit is slightly oval with a purple shell-like rind and three-lobed, serrated leaves. The pulp is juicy and aromatic, with many seeds. Unfortunately it is hard to get as much fruit off of the passion vine as you might like. Even though you may not be able to make juice, this plant is still worth growing for its attractive flowers.

A passion vine bearing fruit.

193

Q I would like to grow a Mexican flame vine near the salt water on the back of my property. Will it take these tough conditions?

A It should. The Mexican flame vine is extremely salt tolerant. It can be propagated from cuttings, and although cold temperatures injure it, the Mexican flame vine normally comes back with an abundance of vigorous vines featuring an orange-red, daisy-shaped flower that blooms much of the year.

Q I recently saw a plant called the golden chalice at a commercial garden. How come I haven't seen this before?

A The golden chalice (*Solandra guttata*) isn't seen much outside of commercial gardens in Florida because it is not very cold hardy. It also needs quite a bit of moisture and a fairly fertile soil to grow well. In the right growing conditions, it can grow flowers up to ten inches long and is certainly a sight to behold.

Q My cape honeysuckle is overpowering me. Is there anything I can do to keep it in check?

A The cape honeysuckle (*Tecomaria capensis*) is a shrubby plant from South Africa that blooms six months out of the year. One drawback, as you have noticed, is that it is extremely aggressive, but it can be trimmed after flowering. I recommend cutting them back one-third to one-half. With a little bit of rooting hormone, these cuttings should be easy to start.

I would love to have a jasmine with a subtle fragrance. What would you suggest?

 The Confederate jasmine (*Jasminum nitidum*), a profuse bloomer beginning in early summer and lasting through the fall, would be a good choice. The vines are normally planted three or four feet apart, although they can spread ten to fifteen feet on their own under the right conditions. The Confederate jasmine has brilliant white, pinwheel-like flowers that have a pleasant fragrance but is not too overpowering. It is mostly seen growing in Central and South Florida, but it will recover from freeze damage in North Florida.

 We grew wisteria in Michigan. Can we also grow it here?

 Wisteria is a vigorous vine that grows to be ten feet or more in height. Although it is not grown as often in Florida as it is in some of the northern states, it can be planted in Central and South Florida. Its dark-green foliage sometimes looks iron deficient when grown in our alkaline soils, so it must be planted in soil improved with peat moss and other organic matter.

Q We have some wisteria planted on the north side of our home. We thought it would be cooler there and the plant would grow better, but it hasn't flowered well at all. Can you help us?

A Wisteria might prefer cooler temperatures, but it still needs full sun to flower well.

Q Our wisteria is in a very dry spot. Should we put some extra irrigation around it?

A If you keep the soil moist, your wisteria will grow much better. Daily watering is essential immediately after planting, then cut back to about an inch a week once the plant takes hold and begins to mature. Vines planted in full sun, of course, require more water than those grown in shady conditions.

Q What ground cover would be best for shady areas?

A There are many ground covers that will fit the bill for those difficult shady areas: English (*Hedera Helix*) or Algerian ivy (*Hedera canariensis*), mondo grass (*Ophiopogon* spp.), dwarf liriope, creeping fig (*Ficus pumila*), ajuga, ferns, and even begonias.

Q I have a sloped area that runs from my sidewalk down about four feet to the side of my building. What can I plant here that won't have to be mowed?

Mondo grass is the perfect ground cover for a sloped, shady area.

A Sloped areas are ideal places for ground covers. For sunny areas you might consider dwarf Confederate jasmine (*Jasminum nitidum*), beach daisy (*Chrysanthemum Leucanthemum*), and honeysuckle (*Lonicera* spp.). Liriope, mondo grass, creeping fig, and Boston fern (*Nephrolepis exaltata* var. 'Bostoniensis') are all options for shady areas.

Q Can I plant ground covers around the base of my trees?

A Ground covers around a tree are always picturesque. Azaleas (*Rhododendron* spp.), which are not considered ground covers, are popularly used this way as well. Liriope and mondo grass make an attractive arrangement around trees, as do vining ground covers such as jasmine, wandering Jew (*Tradescantia albiflora*), or even philodendrons.

Q Our patio is in constant use for parties and other get-togethers. Is there a hardy ground cover I can use between my patio bricks?

A As a matter of fact, there are ground covers ideal for this kind of use in the landscape. The dwarf grasses—zoysia, Bermuda

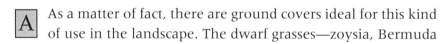

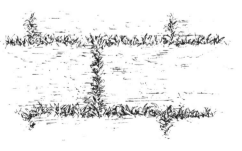

Dwarf grasses are a good ground cover to use between bricks on a patio or walkway.

(*Cynodon Dactylon*), ivy or dwarf mondo (*Ophiopogon* spp.), or monkey grass—are a good example.

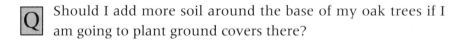

Q Should I add more soil around the base of my oak trees if I am going to plant ground covers there?

A I do not recommend adding too much soil around the base of trees. A couple of inches of soil may not cause problems, but any more than that will. The roots' ability to absorb both water and nutrients will be affected by a soil level change.

Q What do I use to get rid of grass and weeds in an area where I plan to put in a bed of ground covers?

A Round-Up, or another product containing glyphosate, is your best bet. This will kill off the entire bed from the root and leave it virtually free of undesirable growth. For a healthier bed, it is also important to start it off with a quality soil.

Q What is the best time of the year to plant ground cover beds in Florida?

A Since the ground hardly ever freezes here, anytime of the year is fine. Spring is usually the preferred time. Mid-summer can be tough due to the intense heat as can mid-winter due, obviously, to the cold.

Q What type of fertilizer should I use for my ground covers?

A A water-soluble plant fertilizer will give your ground covers a good growing boost. A watering can or hose-end sprayer can be used as an applicator. Fish emulsion is also a popular method of fertilization; it may not smell the best, but it is great for the plants. After your ground covers are well established, a general fertilizer, such as a 6-6-6, 8-8-8, or 10-10-10, will be sufficient.

Q Once I have established a bed of ground covers, how do I keep weeds from invading the beds?

A The most common methods are laying a landscape fabric or mulching beds with two or three inches of mulch. You could also use a mist bottle or wick-type system to apply a light coat of Round-Up or similar herbicide.

11

INSECTS AND DISEASES

Florida is blessed, or you might say cursed, with the ideal climate for insects. This idyllic climate is perfect for year-round gardening and year-round bugs. And there are more bugs out there than you might imagine. There are bugs that can attack your garden, your lawn, your trees, and your shrubs. Of course, there are also some good bugs out there, working to help you control the bad ones. Knowing what's out there crawling around your plants will give you the power to be proactive in your garden. You can win the war, even if occasionally losing a few battles to the beasties.

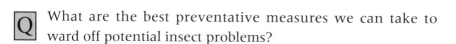

Q What are the best preventative measures we can take to ward off potential insect problems?

A Sometimes good sanitation in and around your yard is the best step. In other words, get rid of leaves that are infected, inspect for insects before they become a major problem, and spray early in the life cycle of insects you find to avoid a severe outbreak.

Eliminating trash areas, which many insects and pests love, and reducing watering levels, which will help cut down on fungus problems, are also good steps to take. Last, planting insect- and disease-resistant varieties of plants will help reduce insects and diseases.

Q I have noticed that many fertilizers are high in nitrogen, but I have heard that this may actually increase some insect and fungus problems. Is this true?

A It is true that a high-nitrogen fertilizer will push lush growth, which in turn, can cause the plant to be more susceptible to not only fungus problems but also caterpillars and other insects. You do need to use a fertilizer that has an adequate amount of nitrogen as well as phosphorous and potassium and other elements, but it is more important to get a good balance with your fertilizer than to push growth with one that is high in nitrogen.

Q We came across a canna that is being bothered by a worm that has curled the leaf up tightly around it. What can we do to get rid of it?

A Cannas normally have problems with this little worm, called a canna leaf roller. It actually curls up in the leaf and eats it. It is somewhat difficult to get rid of completely, but treating with an insecticide such as Sevin should help.

Q If we have problems with our plants, where can we take them for identification?

A You can always go to the county extension office. There is a county extension horticulturist in every county in the state, and they can identify the majority of insect and disease problems for you. If they have a problem, they might send your sample to a specialist in Gainesville where the IFAS (Institution of Food and Agricultural Sciences) has its office. Also, many nurserymen are quite knowledgeable and can usually help as can certified pest control operators.

Q I have came across a large insect that is yellow, red, and black. It looks like a grasshopper, but it is four or five inches long. What is this bug and what do you recommend for its control?

A You are describing the lubber grasshopper. The adults are yellow with black and red markings, and they can grow up to five inches long. The young are black with red or yellow lines, and at this stage they can be treated with a contact insecticide such as Diazinon or Malathion. Often you have to manually kill the adult lubbers. Luckily, these grasshoppers only seem to devour some of the lilies (*Lilium* spp.) and don't come in great enough numbers to cause damage throughout the yard.

Q We recently got some organic dirt that had a tiny insect in it called a spring tail. Should we try to get rid of it?

A Spring tails got their name from their tails that actually spring them forward, throwing their tiny bodies into the air. Since these insects usually feed upon organic matter, it isn't really necessary to control them.

Q We recently watched an amazing insect that had two sets of legs fly around our backyard like a helicopter. Is this something to worry about?

A No doubt what you were looking at was a dragonfly. Dragonflies, in their nymph stage, feed upon some insects that are harmful to plants, so they are considered one of the good guys. They do not hurt humans and are certainly entertaining.

Q I found a leaf on my citrus tree that had tiny eggs, one on top of the other, lined along the margin of the leaf. Do you know what this is?

A This is a katydid. It is typical for their egg pattern to run along the edges of a leaf. Often katydids will feed on citrus and leave a mark on the side of the fruit. Since they do not usually appear in big numbers, katydids are not a major problem. They are also pretty well kept in check by other insects, so no control is recommended for them.

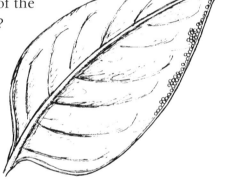

Katydids lay their eggs on the edges of leaves.

Q Our bahia grass has been attacked by thousands of mole crickets. Are they always this bad?

A Mole crickets seem to be worse some years than others. Mole crickets look like field crickets only they have large front legs. They live in the ground and often do much of their tunneling in the night. Because they are attracted to light, mole crickets can be seen in garages and bouncing off porch lights. Spraying with Dursban or Diazinon or using a cricket bait in early spring or summer is often your best line of defense.

 Is it true that the praying mantis is beneficial?

Yes. This odd-looking insect, which can grow two to three inches long, feeds on many other pests in the garden.

We noticed a silky webbing on the trunk of our oak tree. What should we do about this?

This is no doubt the work of a psocid, sometimes called book louse. They are extremely tiny, sometimes only one millimeter in size. They feed on algae off of the tree and are protected by the webbing they produce. Normally, I wouldn't worry about treating for them, but if I am treating the tree for something else, almost any general insecticide will kill them.

Our gardenia has always been bothered by tiny insects that get down into the center of the flower. What is it?

Your gardenia has flower thrips. Thrips are small insects that are usually about one-tenth to one-twenty-fifth of an inch long. They vary in color from black to white to yellow. Thrips are elongated with short antennae and rather large eyes. They suck plant tissue, causing a mottled appearance. Spraying with Diazinon, a systemic, or Malathion should help.

Q We have a sycamore tree that is plagued by a tiny lacy insect. Its leaves are developing a stippled appearance. What is this bug and how do we get rid of it?

A This tiny insect, only about four millimeters long, is the sycamore lace bug. In addition to feasting on the sycamore (*Acer pseudoplatanus*), they also attack hibiscus, azaleas (*Rhododendron* spp.), and oak trees (*Quercus* spp.). Spraying with Diazinon, Malathion, Dursban, or another insecticide labeled for the lace bug should take care of them.

Q We were going to treat our St. Augustine lawn for chinch bugs, but we are not sure if they are the cause of the damage. How can we tell?

A Chinch bug damage is described as looking like a blow torch was used on specific areas of the St. Augustine lawn. The spot will be red to brown. The damage is due to the salivary juices that the bug inserts into the stems of the grass blades. Chinch bug damage often shows itself first in "hot" areas of the lawn—near driveways, sidewalks, or the street. Shady areas will be the last to receive the wrath of the chinch bug. You can control your chinch bugs by spraying with Diazinon, Dursban, or another insecticide labeled specifically for them.

Q I have heard about using a coffee can to detect chinch bugs. How is this done?

A The old practice was to get a coffee can, cut out both ends, then dig the can into the turf about one-inch deep and fill it with water. If you have chinch bugs, you will see them float on the surface of the water the next day.

Q We were in our vegetable garden yesterday and noticed a dark-green insect that had legs that looked like leaves. What is this?

A This is the leaf-footed bug. It is dark green in color with long back legs resembling leaves. They often use their sharp beaks to draw food directly out of the leaves and stems of your (and their) favorite vegetables. Spraying with Sevin, Malathion, or Diazinon will control them.

Q I was walking in my garden and stepped on a large, green bug that had quite a foul odor. What is it, and how can I control it (other than stepping on it)?

A You have met the southern green stink bug, a large, green attacker that emits an extremely unpleasant aroma when crushed. I recommend treatment with Malathion, Diazinon, or Dursban, according to label directions.

Q I noticed some thorny looking insects on my powder puff shrub. Is this something we should be concerned about?

A Thornbugs are certainly unusual with their green color and the tannish-red lines on their backs that make them look like thorns. In great numbers, these cold-sensitive bugs can present serious problems to members of the legume family. Spraying with Diazinon, Malathion, Dursban, or Orthene according to label directions should control them.

Q My citrus, gardenia, and hibiscus are covered with the white fly. How can we get rid of them?

A The white fly and its larvae are a common problem in Florida gardens. In the adult stage, they are tiny (about one-sixteenth of an inch) and pure white. The larvae hatches out from a tiny egg that looks like white specks on the backs of leaves. If you don't notice the eggs, you will notice the black, sooty mold that forms on the leaves from the white fly damage. Spraying on both sides of the foliage with Diazinon, Malathion, Ethion, or Volck oil according to label directions will help you control the flies.

Q Most of the new growth in our garden has aphids. What can we do to eradicate this problem?

A Aphids, also known as plant lice, are tiny, soft-bodied insects that have a sucking mouth part. At their largest, they might be one-sixteenth of an inch. These pear-shaped insects often feed on new growth, which is full of nutrients. The aphid produces large amounts of secretion, sometimes called honeydew. In addition to severely distorting the foliage, a black, sooty mold grows on the secretion left behind. Aphids do not only damage plants as they suck the juices from their leaves, but they can also carry a number of diseases and viruses. If you have aphids, you should spray with Diazinon, Malathion, Dursban, or a soap spray.

Q Our pittosporums have a white, fluffy mass along their stems and leaves. My nurseryman called this cottony cushion scale damage, and he said that it is somewhat difficult to bring under control. Do you have any suggestions?

A Cottony cushion scales attack pittosporums in addition to citrus, aralias, and a number of other ornamental plants. The scales are actually one-quarter of an inch long and reddish-brown, but they are identified by the cottony, white mass they produce to hold their eggs together. This mass is usually a half-inch to three-quarters of an inch long and holds hundreds of eggs. The scales will spread along the leaves and twigs. As your nurseryman said, they are quite difficult to control. The lady bird beetle will help you, as will spraying with Malathion, Diazinon, or Dursban according to label directions.

Q Our sago is always bombarded with a tiny, rounded scale. What should we do about this?

A The hemispherical scale is common on sagos (*Cycas circinalis*), although it also attacks hibiscus, gardenias, ixoras, avocados (*Persea americana*), peaches (*Prunus Persica*), and roses. This scale is normally about one-seventh of an inch long and has a dark brown color, but it is not always easily identified as an insect because its movement is difficult to see. It is tough to get rid of, but spraying with Cygon, Orthene, Dursban, Malathion, or an oil-based combination product should help bring it under control.

Q We have a small grapefruit tree in the backyard, and we are having a hard time controlling the mealy bugs on it. Do you have any suggestions?

A Mealy bugs, like many juice-sucking insects, create secretions that black sooty mold grows on so readily. As with aphids, you might notice ants nearby; they protect the mealy bug because they also feed off of this secretion. Your best defense against these bugs is spraying with Malathion.

Q My podocarpus has a glob of white wax on its stems. What causes this and how can I get rid of it?

A This is, no doubt, the wax scale. It looks just like a drop of white wax. There are also the Indian wax scale and the Florida wax scale, which are slightly smaller. These scales attack a variety of ornamental plants in Florida, such as gardenias, ficus, mangos (*Mangifera indica*), hibiscus, and camellias. You can control this pest by using an oil spray or by applying a systemic such as Cygon or Orthene.

Q Our camellias have white specks on the underside of their leaves. What is this?

A The tea scale is easily the biggest problem for camellias. It presents itself as the whites specks you described, and it sucks the juice from the camellia's leaves, causing severe damage. You will also notice a yellowing on the topside of the foliage. Tea scale is a tough one to control. A thorough application on both sides of the leaves is vital. You will need to use a number of applications of Malathion and oil, Ethion and oil, or Orthene in an attempt to gain control over this difficult scale.

Q I noticed a strange insect in my garden that was covered with bits of leaves and stems. Should I try to control this insect?

A This bizarre insect is sometimes called the trashbug, but it is actually the larvae stage of the lacewing. This insect is an attractive light green color and has golden eyes. The lacewing and its larvae (the trashbug) both feed heavily on mites, scales, and especially, aphids. Obviously, this is a "good guy" insect so no control is recommended. If there were more good guys around, we would do a lot less spraying.

Q We have a lot of little craters in our backyard sand. What causes them and should we do anything about it?

A These craters are usually made by the antlion, or doodlebug. It makes these tiny craters and waits at the bottom for ants and other insects to fall in. It then devours its prey with its clawlike jaws. Like the lacebug, it is a beneficial insect that helps keep damaging insects under control.

Q I enjoy watching the lightening bugs in my yard, but should I be worried about them damaging my plants?

A The lightening bug, or firefly, does attack plants to a minor degree, but they are not normally present in large enough numbers to cause much damage. Besides, like you, most of us enjoy watching their mating ritual of flashing their luminous organs.

Q I found a brown beetle on my back step, and when I accidentally flipped it over with a broom, it jumped into the air and made a clicking sound. Can you tell me what this is?

A You probably won't be surprised to learn that this is called a click beetle. These relatively small beetles are not usually considered a problem. However, the larvae stage, called a wireworm, can be a problem on ornamentals and vegetables. They do not normally attack in great numbers, but if you do have a problem, a general insecticide such as Dursban or Diazinon will help bring them under control.

Q My large Canary Island date palm is being bothered by the palm weevil, and it is so vicious that we can actually hear a chewing noise coming from the trunk. How can we put a stop to this noisy damage?

A This palm weevil is the largest of the Florida weevils, reaching well over an inch in length, but most people do not know that it is present until the palm is gone. If you see these weevils or suspect you have them, call a certified pest control operator. He can treat them with a pesticide such as Dursban or Lindane.

Q I keep seeing an ugly looking caterpillar that resembles bird droppings. What is it?

A This is the orange-dog caterpillar. Its repulsive appearance helps protect it from predators. Since the larvae do feed upon citrus and young trees can be defoliated, spraying with Malathion is recommended. But if you just have an occasional caterpillar, pick off a few of their favorite leaves, put them into a jar with air holes, and watch these ugly ducklings turn into the spectacular swallowtail butterfly.

Q When I was picking up the cuttings from my ixora one day, I felt a sharp pain in my left hand. I looked down to see a beautiful, pale green caterpillar that had two red stripes along its body. Is it possible that this caterpillar stung me?

A   This creature is the IO caterpillar, and its lovely pale green body is covered with long, nettling spines that can sting. These caterpillars often attack oaks (*Quercus* spp.), roses, and willow trees (*Salix* spp.). If you see more than just one caterpillar, spray with Sevin or a contact insecticide such as Diazinon according to label directions.

Q   There is a large, green caterpillar with a pointy end in my poinsettia. What is it and should I get rid of it?

A   The hornworm, which attacks poinsettias (*Euphorbia pulcherrima*) and tomatoes (*Lycopersicon* spp.), is a large caterpillar, growing up to four inches in length. It is not poisonous and does not pose a serious problem, but it can break out in large numbers. If this happens, it will be necessary to spray with Sevin or Thuricide/Biotrol/Dipel (made from the *bacillus thuringiensis*) to keep them from defoliating your plant.

Q   We have oleanders that have been bothered by the oleander caterpillar ever since we planted them. Not only do they eat the oleanders, but they also nest underneath the eaves of our home. What do you recommend?

A   The oleander (*Nerium* spp.) has one major pest: the oleander caterpillar. The larvae of the oleander moth is an orange-colored caterpillar with tufts of black hair scattered over much of its body. The adult stage looks like a wasp and is a dark blue to black in color with white spots on its wings. Because of this coloring, it is sometimes referred to as the polka dot moth. Spraying with the *bacillus thuringiensis* (Dipel/Thuricide/Biotrol) should give you some control.

Q Our cabbage has problems with a large, looping caterpillar that makes it look like Swiss cheese. What can we do?

A The cabbage looper, which can grow to one-and-a-half inches in length, attacks not only cabbage but also broccoli and other greens. Your best line of defense is spraying with Thuricide/Dipel/Biotrol or Diazinon, Malathion, or Orthene on ornamentals.

Q The small seedlings of our tomato plants and other vegetables were cut right at the soil level. When I dug around a couple of these fallen plants, I found a two-inch gray-green caterpillar that was smooth to the touch. What is this?

 A This is the cutworm, and it is the worst problem for vegetables in the state. Placing toothpicks next to the stems of the young seedlings can help cut down on cutworms. Another technique is to cut small pieces of cardboard into circular pieces and make small collars to place around newly planted seedlings; you can also use the insert from a paper towel roll, cut into segments. Spraying with a stomach poison, such as Sevin, or a contact insecticide, such as Diazinon, helps keep the cutworm under control.

Q We have seen a caterpillar in our garden that looks like it is wearing a little brown saddle. Do we need to control it?

A This odd-looking creature is the saddleback caterpillar, also known as a slug caterpillar. It is a problem on many ornamental plants such as palms, roses, and ixoras. It can be controlled by spraying Sevin, Dipel, Malathion, or Dursban according to label directions.

Q I was recently checking some of the leaves from my oak tree and was stung by a caterpillar that looked like a furry dog. What is this thing?

A The furry dog you are describing is the puss caterpillar. It grows to be about one inch long and is covered with brown, silky hairs. Underneath this silky covering are little black spines that sting. They do feed on a number of ornamental trees, including oaks (*Quercus* spp.) and citrus, and are one of the most common stinging caterpillars in Florida. Spray with Sevin, Diazinon, Malathion, or Dursban to get them under control.

Q There are small holes in the side of our St. Augustine's leaves. What causes this damage?

A You have the tropical sod webworm. These green webworms feed during the night, which makes them difficult to find. When you find them, they will be resting in a curved position. Webworms get their name from the silky webbing they create on the grass blades. You can control these by spraying with Dursban, Diazinon, or Dipel/Thuricide/Biotrol.

Q We have been growing tomatoes for a number of years, and it seems as though the leaf miners increase in number every year. How can we get control of this pest?

A The leaf miner is the larval stage (maggot) of a small fly that eats between the upper and lower layers of leaves. This is a serious problem for tomatoes and a number of other vegetables and annual flowers. Spraying with a systemic insecticide, such as

Orthene or Cygon, or a contact insecticide, such as Diazinon or Dursban, will help control them. When spraying on vegetables, be particularly careful about following label directions.

Q We have bugs that curl up into tiny balls in our garden. What are these critters and are they causing any trouble?

A These armored gray bugs, which are not really bugs at all but a member of the Crustacea class, go by many different names, including sowbug, pillbug, and roly-poly. They prefer moist areas and are often found underneath mulch or boards and around potted plants or leaves in the garden. The sowbug does do a slight amount of damage by eating the roots of veggies and plants. If you see them in large numbers, sprinkle Sevin dust or spray with Diazinon or Dursban to control them.

Q We often see slimy trails on our back stoop, heading right toward the garden. What is causing this?

A These are slugs. Their presence is quickly spotted by the slimy trails they leave as they travel across concrete. When they are present in large numbers, you can control them by applying a slug and snail bait, which is available at most nurseries and garden supply stores.

Q We found a little creature in our backyard with two pairs of legs to each body segment. Is this a cause for concern to our plants?

A This is most likely the millipede, which is a wormlike insect with a hard body covering. Millipedes eat dead plant material so they are not considered a problem. If they did occur in severe enough numbers to demand control, Dursban or Diazinon would do the job.

INDEX

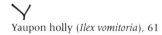